LIFE OF ST. ANTHONY
«ASSIDUA»

D0596512

LIFE OF ST. ANTHONY «ASSIDUA»

by a Contemporary Franciscan

Introduced by
VERGILIO GAMBOSO, O.F.M. Conv.

Translated by
BERNARD PRZEWOZNY, O.F.M. Conv.

emp – Edizioni Messaggero – Padua

I Edition
II Reprint

ISBN   88-7026-552-8

© 1984 Prov. Pad. F.M.C. Editrice
Grafiche Messaggero di S. Antonio

INTRODUCTION

There are two reliable documents which refer he St. Anthony and were written during his lifetime: the short letter he received from St. Francis in 1224, commissioning him to teach theology to the friars, and the account, produced by Thomas of Celano in 1228, describing Francis' miraculous apparitions to friars in Arles while Anthony was preaching to them. Just as reliable, however, are the hagiographies or lives of the saint which were also written in the thirteenth century. They vary in length and importance, but each, in its own way, faithfully describes his life, personality, apostolic activity, and the extraordinary veneration he received from people immediately after his death in 1231.[1]

Chronologically and for its historical value, the *Vita prima* or *Assidua*, as it is often called because of the first word of its prologue, is of primary importance. It was written in Latin, the language of medieval culture, by a Franciscan friar who was St. Anthony's contemporary. Although we don't know his name, he wrote the life by mandate of his Paduan superior and at the request of his confreres, completing it in the very year of the saint's canonization, 1232.

Between 1233 and 1234, Julian of Speyer, a German

---

[1] For more adequate bibliographic information and for the critical edition of the *Assidua*, consult Vergilio Gamboso, *Vita prima di S. Antonio or «Assidua» (c. 1232)*, Padua: EMP - Edizioni Messaggero, 1981.

Franciscan composed the liturgical office for the feast of St. Anthony. Its responsory, *Si quaeris miracula* (If miracles you seek), immediately became a favourite prayer. At the same time, Julian also wrote a beautiful summary of the *Assidua*. Although he didn't add any new information, his summary placed a special accent on Anthony's Franciscan ideals.

Toward 1246, an anonymous friar again summarized and reworked the *Assidua,* this time for an anthology of famous Franciscans. The title of his work is the *Dialogus de gestis sanctorum fratrum Minorum* (Dialogue Concerning the Deeds of Saintly Friars Minor).

At the end of the general chapter of Franciscan superiors, gathered in Padua in 1276, Jerome of Ascoli, the minister general who was to become Pope Nicholas IV, commissioned John Peckham, the former minister provincial of England, theologian at the papal court, and later Archbishop of Canterbury, to write a new life of St. Anthony. To guide him in his work, Peckham was given written testimonies which came from Portugal, southern France and, above all, from the area of Padua and Venice. His new life is known as the *Benignitas*. The outstanding trait of his work is its focus on the miraculous powers which St. Anthony already possessed during his lifetime.

A legend—from the Latin word for a text to be read (*legenda*) in liturgical assemblies and community gatherings—appeared some time towards the end of the century. Commonly called the *Raymundina*, it is important because it gathers the recollections of Anthony's companions and describes the social milieu of Padua during the last months of his life. The work is therefore a witness to the saint's spirituality and to the growing veneration of his countless devotees.

Finally, the *Rigaldina,* written by a Franciscan from Limoges, Johannes Rigaldi or Jean de Rigaud (Rigault), gathers traditions about St. Anthony that were handed down by the older friars of Limoges and southern France.

As we mentioned, the *Assidua* appeared on the occasion of Anthony's canonization in 1232, a year after his death. Although we don't know the name of the author, we can deduce from this life that he was a Franciscan friar. He himself tells us in the prologue that he wrote the work in response to the assiduous requests of his confreres and in obedience to his superiors. Not only his cultural formation, piety and sincere attachment to the Franciscan Order but also his respect for the clergy and particular deference for the bishop of Padua lead us to believe that he originally belonged to the clergy of the diocese and only at a mature age joined the religious community founded by St. Francis. If he was not a Paduan by birth, he became one by adoption. If this is true, then he resembled St. Anthony who was Portuguese. He was obviously a learned man, a well-read person capable of composing artful prose. Furthermore, he was not only an expert in the religious culture of his day but also knew his Bible well.

The *Assidua* was primarily destined for liturgical reading by religious and diocesan clergy, but it was also available to anyone who desired to know the life and miracles of St. Anthony. The writer's sincere devotion led him to write a life which might inspire others to righteous living and bring them to venerate the saint. These reasons explain why he did not digress in superfluous accounts but narrated only what was indispensable for the piety of readers. In humble fulfillment of his task, he remained silent about himself and also clothed Anthony in a mantle of secrecy out of respect for his modesty and interior life with God.

The writer tells us that he was not an eyewitness to some of the events he describes, but that he relied on information supplied, either orally or in writing, by the bishop of Lisbon and other people worthy of trust. He reminds us that, in similar circumstances, other writers followed the same procedure. He cites the exemples of the evangelists Mark and Luke, and of Pope St. Gregory the Great. We presume that he had asked for and received information from John Parenti, the minister general from 1227 to 1232, who was the former provincial of the Iberian peninsula and may have personally welcomed the Augustinian canon who became St. Anthony into the Franciscan Order.

Knowing that God must be praised and the saint should be venerated, the author chose the death of Anthony as the event around which to organize his literary work. It is at this critical moment that the saint definitively professed his faith in God, and the miracles which immediately followed his death were signs of God's pleasure with his whole life. Thus, all praise belongs to God and the saint was revealed to be worthy of veneration. The *Assidua* is therefore divided into two parts, each subdivided into short chapters with summary headings. The first part recalls the more important events in his life; the second describes his death, the circumstances of his burial and canonization, and lists the miracles. The outline, with the accompanying numbered chapters, is the following:

1. General prologue (1);
2. First Part: life and deeds (2-15);
3. Second Part: prologue (16); death, burial, canonization (17-29); prologue to the miracles (30); the 53 miracles presented at the canonization (31-46); epilogue (47, 1-3);
4. General epilogue (47, 4-6).

Vergilio Gamboso, O.F.M.Conv.

TRANSLATOR'S NOTE

As far as I am aware, this is the first translation of the *Assidua* from Latin into English. Not only its interest for St. Anthony's clients but also its value for students of early Franciscanism warranted the undertaking.

Every translator exposes himself to criticism whenever he «interprets» the original to produce a readable text. In the case of a medieval work, he runs the risk whenever he must translate nouns as subordinate clauses; and, he must do this more often than is usually required by the ablative absolute of classical Latin.

I found Vergilio Gamboso's Italian translation of great help in avoiding many pitfalls, but I couldn't always accept his «interpretation» because English syntax permitted a more literal reading.

Bernard Przewozny, O.F.M.Conv.

CONTENTS

FIRST PART

SECOND PART

MIRACLES

THE BEGINNING OF THE FIRST PART

1. - HERE BEGINS THE PROLOGUE
   TO THE LIFE OF BLESSED ANTHONY

1. Guided by the insistent demand of friars and inspired by the merit of sanctifying obedience, for the praise and glory of almighty God, and to satisfy the love and devotion of the faithful, I am led to write about the life and deeds of the most blessed father and our confrere Anthony. 2. In a «life» of saints, everything is transmitted in writing to a future generation of believers so that, having heard of the miraculous signs which God works in them, the Lord may always and in all things be praised, and to the faithful there may be offered a norm of right living with an incentive to devotion.

3. Although I know that I am quite incompetent for such a task, I nonetheless do not restrain my lips, trusting that he who sees the intention of my heart will bring my undertaking to completion. 4. Thus, I speak succinctly to the followers of Christ, guided only by truth, that is, by simple terms, lest the eloquent loquaciousness of words only serve itching ears and, consequently, men be satisfied with the mere turning of pages.

5. Many of the things I write about I did not see with my own eyes, but I came to know them

from my Lord Sugerius,[1] bishop of Lisbon, and from other Catholic men who told me about them. 6. In the same way, Mark and Luke wrote their gospels. Thus, also, Gregory wrote his *Dialogues* (in which Peter is a questioner): he himself tells us that he learned what he wrote only from the account of men who were trustworthy.

7. So that the faithful who read this life may more easily find what they are looking for, I have divided this work into two parts and have added a summary subtitle to each one of the chapters. 8. In the first part, I have described some of the better known events of his life, choosing them, for the sake of brevity, from among the many which occurred after his first acceptance of the religious habit. 9. In the second part, then, relying on the testimonies of our friars and other trustworthy faithful, I have gathered the marvels that God worked through him.

10. I, who wrote this life, exhort the reader that he not accuse me of lying or of falsehood but mercifully recognize my ignorance or forgetfulness when he reads and finds that in some place I said too little, or that in another I exceeded the limits of truth because of my incautious choice of words.

HERE ENDS THE PROLOGUE AND BEGINS
THE LIFE OF BLESSED ANTHONY

---

[1] Sugerius II Viegas, bishop of Lisbon from 1210 to 1232, travelled to Rome in 1231 when the canonical procedures for Anthony's canonization were already initiated.

Camposampiero, Padua: The shrine of the «Nut Tree» where St. Anthony spent the last days of his life, from May to June 13, 1231. The church was frescoed by Girolamo Tessari and his disciples between 1530 and 1540.

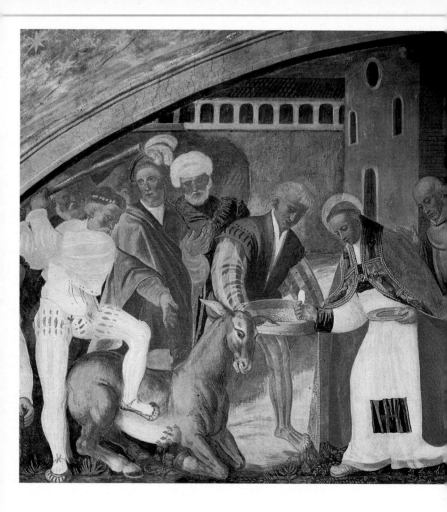

St. Anthony accepts a heretic's challenge. A donkey, which had not been fed for three days, refused to eat hay; instead, it fell to its knees in adoration before the Eucharist.

St. Anthony preaches from the nut tree.

St. Anthony preached so eloquently before Pope Gregory IX that the latter called him «The Ark of the Testament.»

A precious ring, lost at sea, was found through St. Anthony's intercession within a fish that had swallowed it.

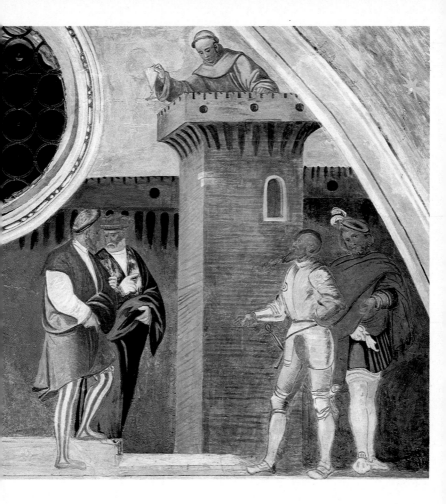

The miracle of the unbroken glass.

A nobleman is saved through the intercession of St. Anthony.

2. - CONCERNING THE CITY OF BLESSED ANTHONY

1. I have been told that there is a certain city in the kingdom of Portugal, situated in its western regions at the extreme limits of the world. It is called Ulixbone[1] by its inhabitants because it is commonly thougth to have been founded by Ulysses. 2. Within its walls, there stands a church[2] of admirable size built to the honour of the glorious Virgin Mary. In this church rests the precious body of the blessed martyr Vincent,[3] guarded with all honour and worthy of every veneration.

3. The fortunate parents of Anthony[4] owned at the west side of this district a house worthy of their social condition, its entrance being close to the threshold of the church. 4. They were in the first flower of their youth when they begot this fortunate child and gave him the name Ferdinand at the holy font of baptism.

5. Indeed, they entrusted him to this church, dedicated to the holy Mother of God, so that he learn the sacred writings[5] there, and, as if led by a presentiment, they confided the future herald of Christ to the education of Christ's ministers.

---

[1] Lisbon.
[2] The reference is to the Cathedral of Lisbon which still exists today. It has preserved the font where Ferdinand was baptized.
[3] The deacon Vincent of Saragossa was martyred during the persecution of Emperor Diocletian (c. 304).
[4] Martin Alphonse de' Buglioni and Mary.
[5] The Bible and basic Christian doctrine.

3. - HOW HE ENTERED
THE ORDER OF ST. AUGUSTINE

1. Having, therefore, serenely spent his childhood years at home, he happily completed his fifteenth birthday. 2. At puberty, although disordinate passions of the flesh increased and he felt himself tormented beyond normal, he never relaxed his watchfulness over adolescence and sensual pleasures. Instead, mastering the weak human condition, he tightened the reins over the impulses of carnal concupiscence. 3. In everyday affairs, the world seemed foolish to him and he withdrew his foot from its threshold before he had fully stepped onto it, fearing that in some way the dust of earthly joys might adhere to him and create an obstacle for one who, in spirit, was already running quickly along the Lord's way.

4. Not too far from the walls of the abovementioned city, there stands a monastery of the Order of St. Augustine[6] in which live men who are known for their religious observance, dedicated to the Lord in the habit of the Canons Regular. 5. To this place, then, once he set aside the delights of the world, came the man of God and, with humble devotion, took the habit of the Canons Regular.

6. He lived there for almost two years, putting up with the frequent visits of friends which so disturb pious souls. To remove every such occasion of disturbance, he decided to leave his native region—something that can annoy even manly souls to no small degree—so that he might serve the Lord

---

[6] The Canonia di São Vicente and its church were rebuilt after the earthquake of 1775.

more peacefully, sheltered by the ramparts of an un-known shore. 7. And, after many requests, as soon as he obtained the superior's permission, he changed not the order but his residence, moving with lively fervour to the monastery of the Holy Cross in Coimbra.

4. - HOW HE PROGRESSED
IN VIRTUE AND LEARNING IN COIMBRA

1. Inspired, therefore, by love for a more se-vere form of discipline and more fruitful tranquility, the servant of God moved to the monastery of the Cross. His growing fervour showed that he had changed not so much his place as his habitual con-duct. 2. And, since a text says, «it is not having been to Jerusalem but having lived there well that is praiseworthy,» so he showed himself in possession of such virtues that it was clearly apparent to all that he had searched for a more appropriate place where he might reach the height of perfection.
3. He always cultivated his innate talents with special eagerness and exercised his mind with medi-tation. Day and night, whenever the occasion arose, he would not neglect to read the Scriptures. 4. In reading the Bible with attention to its historical truth, he also strengthened his faith with allegorical comparisons; and, in applying the words of the Scriptures to himself, he edified his affections with virtues.
5. In examining, out of healthy curiosity, the deep sense of God's words, he protected his intel-lect with scriptural testimonies against the pitfalls of error. For this reason, he often returned to the words of the saints with diligent inquiry. 6. And,

indeed, he entrusted to his tenacious memory whatever he read, so that in a short time he was able to acquire a knowledge of the Scriptures that no one else hoped to possess.

5. - HOW, MOVED BY THE DESIRE OF MARTYRDOM,
    BLESSED ANTHONY ENTERED THE
    ORDER OF FRIARS MINOR AND
    CONCERNING HIS CHANGE OF NAME

1. Later, when Peter, the Lord Infante, brought from Morocco the relics of the holy Franciscan martyrs [7] and made known throughout all the provinces of Spain that he had been miraculously freed by their merits, the servant of God, hearing of the miracles that were being performed by them, was also guided by the fortitude of the Holy Spirit and, girding his flanks with the belt of faith, strengthened his arm with the weapon of divine zeal. 2. He used to say within his heart, «If only the Most High would deign to make me share in the crown of his holy martyrs! If only the executioner's sword would strike me as I, on bended knee, offer him my neck for the name of Jesus! Will I see this come about? Will I reach that moment of great joy?» He would silently say these and similar things to himself.

3. At that time, not far from the city of Coimbra, some Friars Minor lived in a place that was called Saint Anthony. [8] Although they were not learned men, they taught the substance of the Scrip-

---

[7] These are the first Franciscan martyrs who were killed on January 16, 1220: Berard, Peter, Accursius, Adiutus, and Otto.

[8] St. Anthony de Olivais stood on a hill covered with olive trees.

tures with their actions. 4. They, according to the norms of their order, would often come to beg for alms at the monastery where the man of God lived.

5. As usual, the man of God approached them one day so that he might converse with them alone. Of the many things he spoke about, he also said, «Dearest brothers, with a willing spirit I would put on the habit of your order if you were to promise to send me, as soon as I join, to the land of the Saracens so that I, too, might merit with the holy martyrs to receive a share in the crown.» 6. The friars, filled with great joy by the words of such a man, decided that this be done on the day after the next, and, lest their delaying cause inconvenience, they took immediate action.

7. Thus, while the friars were happily returning home, the servant of God remained to seek the abbot's permission for what he had decided. 8. Indeed, he had hardly wrested it after many entreaties, when the friars, not having forgotten his promise, came early in the morning according to their agreement and very quickly in the monastery vested the servant of God in the habit of their order.

9. As soon as the vesting was completed, one of his confreres and canons ran up and spoke out of the bitterness of his heart, saying, «Go, go, because now you will be a saint!» 10. The man of God humbly said to him, «Very well, when you hear it said that I'm a saint, you will praise God for it.» 11. And, having said this, the friars quickly hurried home and welcomed with signs of affection the new guest who had followed their footsteps.

12. Inasmuch as the servant of God feared the violent reaction of his relatives who tried to seize him, he very cleverly made every effort to elude

their diligent searching for him. 13. In fact, having changed his former name, he himself adopted that of Anthony, thus giving a sign of how great a herald of God's word he would become. 14. Indeed, «Anthony» more or less means «high sounding.» And, truly, when he spoke to the learned of God's wisdom hidden in mystery, his voice like a strong trumpet proclaimed so many and such profound truths of the Bible that even a person who was accustomed to scriptural interpretation could rarely understand his eloquence.

6. - HOW HE WENT TO MOROCCO
AND CONCERNING HIS RETURN

1. His zeal for the spread of the faith urged him on ever more earnestly and his thirst for martyrdom, which burned in his heart, never gave him rest. 2. And, so, according to the promise made to him, it happened that, as soon as he obtained permission, he hastily left for the land of the Saracens.[9]

3. But, the Most High, who knows what is in man, opposed his projects and, striking him with a grave illness, punished him very painfully throughout the winter. 4. When he saw that he could do nothing to bring to fulfillment what he had proposed, it dawned on him that to recover at least his bodily health he had to return to his native land.

5. During the voyage, just as he was ready to land in Spain, he saw himself carried by strong winds to the shores of Sicily.[10] 6. About that

---

[9] Morocco.

[10] Later traditions speak of Taormina or Milazzo as the ports where he landed in Sicily.

time, it was decided to celebrate a general chapter in Assisi. [11] When the servant of God was informed of this by the friars of the city of Messina, showing himself stronger than he really was, he reached the place of the chapter as best he could.

7. - HOW HE CAME TO ROMAGNA
AND HOW HE LIVED THERE

1. Once the chapter was concluded as usual, and when the ministers provincial had sent the friars entrusted to them to their destinations, only Anthony remained abandoned in the hands of the minister general, not being requested by anyone of the other ministers, like a man who is considered inexperienced and of little use, and because he was not even known. 2. At last, when he called apart Friar Gratian, who was then governing the friars in Romagna, the servant of God began to entreat him that, once released by the minister general, he be taken to Romagna and there be taught the rudiments of their spiritual life.

3. He neither mentioned his studies nor boasted of the churchly ministry he had exercised; instead, out of love for Christ, hiding all his knowledge and intelligence, he declared that he wished to know, thirst for, and embrace only Christ, and him crucified.

4. Friar Gratian, having esteemed his admirable devotion, assented therefore to the wishes of the man of God and, taking him with himself, brought him to Romagna. 5. When Anthony, through God's disposition, reached the place, he devoutly

---

[11] The Pentecost Chapter of 1221.

retired, after he had obtained permission, to the hermitage of Monte Paolo[12] where he entered into the peace of silence.

6. While Anthony was staying in that hermitage, a certain friar built himself a cell in a grotto which was suitable for prayer and where he could dedicate himself more freely to God. 7. When the man of God saw it one day and realized how appropriate it was for growth in devotion, he went to entreat the friar and humbly asked him to cede to him the use of that cell. 8. At last, when he obtained the place of peace, the servant of God, after fulfilling the morning community prayers, would daily retire to the cell, taking with himself some bread and a small container of water. 9. In this way, he spent the day alone, forcing the body to serve the spirit; but, in observance of the holy norms, he always returned on time for the friars' reunion.

10. Often, when the bell rang, he would prepare to return to the friars, but, since his body was tired out by sleeplessness and weakened by abstinence, he would walk uncertainly, waver, and fall. 11. Indeed, sometimes he so reined in the desires of his flesh with abstinence that, unless he had been held up by the friars (someone who was present is a witness to this), he would not have been able to walk back to the hermitage.

8. - HOW HIS LEARNING WAS NOTED BY THE FRIARS

1. At the end of some time,[13] it happened that friars were to be sent to the city of Forlì to receive

---

[12] Montepaolo is 400 meters (some 437 yards) above sea level, close to Forlì.

[13] About a year later.

holy orders. 2. For this reason, when Franciscan and Dominican friars had gathered there from different parts, Anthony was among them.

3. As the time of the ordination approached and the friars were gathered together as usual, the local minister began to ask the Dominican friars who were present to address an exhortation to those thirsting for the word of salvation. 4. But, when each one began to say quite resolutely that he neither wanted nor ought to preach something improvised, then the superior turned to Friar Anthony and ordered him to proclaim to those who were assembled whatever the Holy Spirit might suggest to him.

5. The superior did not believe that Anthony knew any part of the Scriptures nor thought that he had read anything beyond, perhaps, what concerned the Church's Office. He trusted only one indication, that is, he had heard Anthony speak Latin when necessity required it. 6. In truth, although Anthony was so industrious that he relied on his memory rather than on books, and although he abundantly overflowed with the grace of mystical language, the friars nonetheless knew him as more skillful in washing kitchen utensils than in expounding the mysteries of Scripture.

7. Why say anything else? Anthony resisted as much and as long as he could. At last, because of the loud insistence of all those present, he began to speak with simplicity. But when that writing reed of the Holy Spirit (I am referring to Anthony's tongue) began to speak of many topics prudently, in quite a clear manner and using few words, then the friars, struck by wonder and admiration, listened to the orator attentively and unanimously. 8. Indeed, the

unexpected depth of his words increased their astonishment; but, to no lesser degree, the spirit with which he spoke and his fervent charity edified them. 9. Filled with holy consolation, they all respected the virtue of humility, accompanied by the gift of knowledge, that was manifest in the servant of God.

9. - CONCERNING HIS PREACHING IN ROMAGNA AND ON THE CONVERSION OF HERETICS

1. Inasmuch as, according to the Lord's saying, «a city built on a mountain cannot be hidden,» shortly thereafter the minister was informed of what happened. Anthony, therefore, broke his peaceful silence and was constrained to turn to the public. 2. When the duty of preaching was imposed on him, the faithful dweller of the hermitage was sent out into the world and his lips, closed for so long, were opened to proclaim the glory of God. 3. Sustained, then, by the authority of the one who sent him, he strove so much to fulfill his work of preaching that he merited for his strenuous efforts the title of «Evangelist.» Accordingly, going about cities and castles, villages and countrysides, he sowed the seed of life most abundantly and fervently.

4. As he moved from one place to another, utterly denying himself any rest because of his zeal for souls, it happened that by heavenly inspiration he reached the city of Rimini. Since he saw there many people deceived by perverse heresy, he soon called together all the inhabitants of the city and began to preach fervently. Although he was not versed in the subtleties of philosophers, he confounded the cun-

ning doctrines of the heretics more lucidly than the sun. 5. His powerful words and salutary doctrine so rooted themselves in the hearts of his listeners that, when the defilement of error was eliminated, a large crowd of believers adhered faithfully to the Lord.

6. Among these, there was a heretic by the name of Bononillo [14] who was for thirty years seduced by error into disbelief. Through his servant Anthony, the Lord brought him back to the path of truth. Once he accepted to do penance, he devoutly obeyed the commandments of the Holy Roman Church until the end.

10. - CONCERNING HIS FAME
AND THE EFFICACY OF HIS PREACHING

1. At the conclusion of this, when the minister of the order sent the servant of God to the papal curia beacuse of an urgent matter concerning the religious family, the Most High gave him such favour among the venerable princes of the Church that his sermons were heard with the warmest devotion by the supreme pontiff [15] and by the whole assembly of cardinals. 2. Indeed, with fluent words, he drew out of Scripture such original and profound meanings that he was called by the pope himself, with a phrase all his own, «The Ark of the Testament.»

3. His preaching, seasoned with the salt of grace, conferred abundant divine grace on his lis-

---

[14] Bartholomew of Pisa, writing in the fourteenth century, claims that this is the Bononillo who owned the donkey which fell to its knees in adoration before the Eucharist.

[15] This probably occurred in 1230. The Pope is Gregory IX.

teners. 4. The more respectable marvelled that a man who had barely outgrown puberty and who was uncultured could subtly adapt spiritual things to spiritual men; the less respectable were stunned how he plucked out the causes and occasions of sins and how with greater care he sowed the practice of virtue. 5. Men of every condition, class, and age were happy to have received from him admonitions suitable for their lives.

6. The social status of people did not influence him at all; no flattering opinion of men charmed him. But, according to the words of the prophet, like a threshing cart equipped with searing prows, he crushed mountains and reduced hills to dust.

11. - HOW HE CAME TO PADUA
AND PREACHED THERE

1. Since it would take too much space to relate the many provinces through which he had travelled and how many parts of the earth he had filled with the seed of God's word, we set our hands on those things which necessarily present themselves of greater importance and give much more evident proof of his virtues.

2. At the time of the general chapter when the most holy relics of blessed father Francis were carried to the church where they repose and are duly venerated,[16] the servant of God was released from the government of the friars[17] and received from the

---

[16] This took place on the Vigil of Pentecost, May 25, 1230. The relics of St. Francis were buried in the lower Basilica in Assisi.

[17] He was the minister provincial of Northern Italy, which included the Romagna region.

minister general [18] full freedom to preach. 3. And, since on a previous occasion, that is, when he was writing the sermons for the Sundays of the year, [19] he resided in the city of Padua, [20] and, because he was familiar with the sincere faith of its citizens whom he had fastened to himself with a strong bond of charity, he therefore was drawn by their devotion and decided to visit them at the beginning of his freedom.

4. Later, when by divine consent he reached the city of Padua and had preached there from time to time, he decided to apply his mind fully to study during all of winter. At the request of the bishop of Ostia, [21] he dedicated himself to the writing of sermons for the feasts of saints in the yearly liturgical cycle. 5. While the servant of God was busy with such matters of use to his neighbours, the season of Lent approached. Seeing, therefore, that the acceptable time and the day of salvation drew near, he set aside the work he had begun and again directed all his attention to preaching to the people who thirsted for God's word.

6. So great a desire to preach inflamed him that he decided to do so for the next forty days. [22] Truly, he did just that. 7. And, it certainly arouses wonder since a man, who was afflicted by a certain natural bulkiness and furthermore suffered

---

[18] John Parenti.

[19] These sermons are compositions which embrace theology, pastoral care, and preaching.

[20] St. Anthony came to Padua in 1229.

[21] Rinaldo, bishop of Ostia between 1231 and 1232, became Pope Alexander IV in 1254.

[22] Uninterrupted daily preaching during Lent was a novel form of apostolate begun by Anthony himself.

from continual sickness, nevertheless, out of untiring zeal for souls, persevered in preaching, teaching and listening to confessions until sunset, and often without having eaten.

12. - CONCERNING THE DEVIL'S PERSECUTION AND THE MIRACLE OF LIGHT

1. Since he is jealous of virtue, the ancient enemy never ceases to place obstacles in the way of good works. Thus, wanting to distract the servant of God from his commitment to salvation, he persisted in provoking Anthony with nocturnal illusions. 2. I will describe a real event which was revealed to a certain friar by God's saint himself, while he was still alive.

3. One night, at the beginning of the Lenten apostolate of which we spoke, as he slept to give rest to his tired limbs, behold the devil dared to squeeze violently the throat of the servant of God and, thus exerting pressure on him, tried to choke him. [23] 4. But Anthony, having invoked the name of the glorious Virgin and having made a sign of the life-giving cross on his forehead, put to flight the enemy of mankind and immediately felt alleviated. 5. And, since he wanted to see the fleeing devil, he opened his eyes. Behold, the whole cell in which he slept was gleaming, made brilliant by a heavenly light. We are certain beyond a doubt that the light descended into the cell by divine power and that the dweller in darkness departed confused, not being able to support its rays.

---

[23] The devil may have provoked a kind of lung paralysis.

13. - CONCERNING THE PADUANS' DEVOTION AND THE RESULTS OF HIS PREACHING

1. As soon as the servant of God saw the door of preaching open to him and the people flock from everywhere in a swollen mass, like a parched terrain in need of water, he decided to meet them daily in the churches of the city. But, because of the multitude of men and women who gathered, and because the size of the churches was by no means large enough to hold so many people, whose number always grew, he withdrew to the wide spaces of open meadows.

2. Crowds of men and women that could hardly be counted came from cities, castles and villages which surrounded Padua, all of them thirsting to hear most devoutly the word of life, and, with firm hope, ready to set their salvation on his sound teaching. 3. Rising in the middle of the night, they contended with each other to come early, and, with burning lamps, hurried most fervently to the place where he would preach. 4. You could see knights and noble matrons running through the darkness of night. People, who were normally accustomed to spend not a small part of the day warming their limbs in soft beds, stretched out in torpor, now you might say kept awake without any discomfort, attentively staring at the preacher's face.

5. The old walked and the young ran, men and women of every age and condition. All set aside their ornaments and dressed, as I might say, in religious habits. 6. Indeed, the venerable bishop of Padua, [24] with all his clergy, followed devoutly the

---

[24] Iacopo di Corrado was the bishop of Padua from 1229 to 1239.

servant of God as he preached and, becoming a model of zeal for his flock, admonished everyone to listen to him by his own example of humility.

7. One and all listened to what he was saying with such willingness that, although often thirty thousand men—as it is reported—were present at a discourse, neither a noise nor a murmur was heard from so large a crowd, but all, as if one person, followed the speaker in continual silence, attentive spiritually and bodily. 8. Also merchants, or those who kept shops of whatever kind for the sale of goods, moved by a great desire to hear him, would not display their wares to passersby until the sermon was finished.

9. Women, inflamed with devotion, would bring scissors with them and try to cut off pieces of his habit as if it were a relic; whoever could touch but the hem of his habit considered himself fortunate. 10. It would not have been possible to protect him from the onrushing throng if he had not been surrounded by a large group of strong young men, of if he did not quickly flee to another place, or, still, if he did not wait until the crowd departed.

11. He called back to brotherly peace those who disagreed with each other and gave freedom to those who were imprisoned. He required that whatever was taken in usury or through violence be restituted. It reached the point that many, having mortgaged houses and fields, placed the money at his feet and, with his counsel, gave back to those who had been defrauded whatever had been gained by extortion or bribery. 12. He freed prostitutes from sinful and disgraceful activities and restrained thieves, notorious for their misdeeds, from coming into illegal contact with what belonged to others. In

this manner, having happily reached the end of the forty days of Lent, he gathered through his zeal a harvest that was pleasing to the Lord.

13. I cannot pass over in silence how large a number of people, both men and women, he induced to confess their sins so that neither friars nor other priests—and not a small group of the latter followed him everywhere—were sufficient to hear their confessions. 14. And some of those who came to do penance would say that they were warned by a divine vision and sent to Anthony with the order to accept his advice in all things. 15. After his death, other people, confiding in the friars, affirmed that blessed Anthony appeared to them during sleep and revealed the names of the friars to whom he was sending them.

14. - HOW HE FORETOLD HIS OWN DEATH

1. Anthony, the glorious confessor of the Lord, knew long before his death when it would occur. But, so as not to cause his confreres any sorrow, he would hide his imminent bodily death by carefully dissimulating it.

2. About fifteen days before he paid the debt of all flesh, as he was admiring the agreeable plain of Padua from a certain hill where he found himself, he exulted in spirit and extolled in wonderful praise the location of the city. 3. Then, turning to the friar who had accompanied him on the trip, he foretold that it would shortly receive a great honour. He did not intimate in any way, however, what the honour would be or by whom it would be conferred. 4. Indeed, we believe the honour of the city of Padua to be no other than the merits of Anthony's holi-

ness, by means of which it would soon become famous. And we already see it exalted by praise which is as admirable as it is unusual.

15. - CONCERNING THE CELL HE ASKED TO BE BUILT IN THE NUT TREE

1. It occurred that, while these things were happening, harvest-tide drew close. 2. The faithful and prudent servant of God, seeing therefore that the people would have to give themselves to the work of gathering the crops, resolved to stop preaching until the time was right again. Thus, when he had dismissed the crowds, he looked for a solitary place. He set out for the locality which is called Camposampiero,[25] hoping to find peaceful seclusion there.

3. A certain nobleman by the name of Tiso was extremely happy at his coming and devoutly showed all earnest signs of courtesy toward the man of God. He held in possession the friars' hermitage. 4. Not too far from the friars' dwelling, this nobleman had a thick forest, where, among other trees, there grew a tall nut tree, from the trunk of which six limbs reached toward the sky to form a kind of crown with its branches. 5. One day, when the servant of God saw its extraordinary beauty, he soon decided—led by the Spirit—that a cell be made for him in the nut tree because the place offered suitable solitude and the kind of rest which is conducive to contemplation.

6. As soon as the friars brought this to the attention of the nobleman, he prepared with his own

---

[25] A large town not far from Padua.

20

hands a cell of mats by binding together piles in the form of a square and transversally to the branches. He also made cells, similar in structure, for his two companions,[26] preparing with greater care the higher cell for the saint's use and the others with lesser attention, according to the wish of the friars. 7. In this cell, the servant of God led a truly solitary life and dedicated himself to exercises of holy contemplation. 8. In short, it proved to be his last dwelling among mortals; by climbing into it, he showed that he was drawing near to heaven.

HERE ENDS THE FIRST PART

---

[26] These were Blessed Luke Belludi and Roger.

THE BEGINNING OF THE SECOND PART

16. - PROLOGUE

1. In the preceding part of our work, which we were able to bring to conclusion by the grace and goodness of the Most High, we wrote with humble devotion, but also after ascertaining the truth, of the life and deeds of our most blessed father and confrere, Anthony. 2. In the part that follows, we give an account of what ought to be added about the marvelous things which the Lord God of majesty deigned to work around him and through him, from the day of his death and thereafter.

3. Truly, since we could not come to know everything and so as not to cause annoyance to readers because of the sea of miracles to be narrated, we propose to set down only those things which seem more necessary in order that the devotion of the faithful be moved with these to divine praise. Those who desire to say more for the edification of faith may always find out from others what they ought to add.

17. - THE DEATH OF BLESSED ANTHONY

1. In the year of our Lord's incarnation 1231, in the fourth indiction, on the thirteenth day of

June, the sixth of the week, the most blessed father and our confrere Anthony, Iberian by origin, in the city of Padua where the Most High exalted his own name through him, in the dwelling of the friars at Arcella, having set forth on the journey of all flesh, happily passed on to the mansions of the heavenly spirits.

2. When for some time he had left behind the crowds of people who flocked together from everywhere to hear and see him, he withdrew, for reasons of rest, from the city of Padua to Camposampiero, and began to give himself exclusively to God. If any dust from his frequent contacts with people in the world had adhered to him, as is usual, he wanted to wipe it off with the tears of devotion and with the hair of holy meditation.

3. When, on a certain day,[1] called by the bell for lunch, he came down from his cell, which he had asked to be built in the nut tree, he sat down at the table with the friars as was his custom. 4. But the hand of the Lord descended on him there, and he suddenly began to be forsaken by the powers of his whole body. As the infirmity increased noticeably, he rose from the table, supported by the friars, but, not being able to hold up his weak limbs, he quickly laid himself on a straw bed.[2]

5. The servant of God, feeling therefore that his bodily death was imminent, called to himself one of his confreres and companions, a certain Roger, and said to him, «Brother, if you agree, I would like to go to Padua, to the place of St. Mary, in order not to burden these friars.» 6. When the

---

[1] June 13, 1231.
[2] He was overcome by a seizure of some kind.

23

brother was persuaded, and a cart had been brought, the holy father was placed on it, although the local friars were opposed as much as possible that he be taken anywhere else. 7. But, since they saw that the most blessed Anthony wished this, they unwillingly gave in to what was being done.

8. Friar Vinotus, who was on his way to visit the man of God, met him when he was already approaching the city. When he saw that Anthony was grievously suffering from the malady, he began to beseech him to stop at the house of the friars at Arcella. In fact, friars lived there next to the monastery of the Poor Ladies, taking care of their spiritual needs, according to the custom of the order. 9. Then, the same friar added that a great tumult and not a bit of confusion would occur at the friars' place once they entered the city because they would be exposed to the troublesome onrush of people. 10. Hearing these things, the servant of God assented to the requests of the petitioner and, acquiescing to his wishes, changed his direction for the friars' house.

11. Once he found himself with the friars at Arcella, the hand of the Lord weighed heavier on him and, as the malady grew more violent, he showed signs of intense anguish. When he had rested for a brief moment, having confessed and received absolution, he began to sing a hymn to the glorious Virgin, saying, «O glorious Lady,» etc.

12. Having finished the hymn, he suddenly raised his eyes toward heaven and, with a stunned look, stared in front of himself for a long time. When the friar who was supporting him asked what he saw, he answered, «I see my Lord.»

13. The friars who were present, seeing that

his happy end was approaching, decided to anoint the saint of God with the oil of holy unction. 14. When a certain friar came to him, carrying the sacred oil as usual, blessed Anthony looked straight at him and said, «Brother, it is not necessary to do this to me, for I already have this anointing within me. Nonetheless, it is good for me and I agree to it.»

15. And, having extended his hands and then joined his palms, he sang the penitential psalms with the friars until he completed them to the end. He still held up for almost half an hour. Then, that most holy soul, freed from the prison of his flesh, was absorbed into the abyss of light.

16. Truly, his body bore altogether the appearance of someone sleeping. And, even his hands, having become very white, surpassed the beauty of their former complexion. His other bodily limbs proved to be flexible, conforming to the touch of those who handled them.

17. O truly holy servant of the Most High, you merited even during this life, to see the Lord! O most holy soul, even if a persecutor's cruelty did not carry you away, nevertheless the desire of martyrdom and the sword of compassion transfixed you a thousand times over! Worthy father, welcome kindly those who honour you with the sacrifices of their devotion, and, through your intercession, help us who are still not allowed to draw close to the face of God. Amen.

18. - CONCERNING THE BOYS' SHOUTING, THE ONRUSH OF THE PEOPLE AND THEIR GRIEF

1. Although the friars tried most diligently and carefully to hide his happy death from strangers, and even from friends and acquaintances, so that they would not be crushed by the onrush of large crowds of people, groups of boys nevertheless ran about the city, shouting, «The holy father is dead! Saint Anthony is dead!» 2. The people, hearing this, ran in massed throngs to Arcella and, completely forgetting the work with which they were supposed to earn their living, surrounded the friars' place like bees.

3. The first to run there quickly, as if flying, were the inhabitants of Capo di Ponte.[3] Reaching the place in a large crowd and with many strong young men, they quickly placed armed guards around the convent. Then, members of religious orders presented themselves. Next, there rushed a mixed crowd of both sexes, young men and maidens, the old and young, the insignificant and important, free and serfs. 5. With one voice and unanimous grief of heart, they all began to lament and show their sincere affection with repeated sighs and tears.

6. They would cry aloud, «Where are you going, father, to return no more? Father of Padua, its chariot and charioteer? Where are you going without your children, o venerable father? Who else will be found like you, a true herald of God's word to us, your orphans? Through the Gospel, you be-

---

[3] The reference is to a surburb which, at that time, existed around the Molino bridge, north of the city of Padua.

got us in Christ Jesus.» 7. In this manner, and precisely so, the general anguish of all and the sadness of each moved the souls of onlookers with unending sighs and loud cries to join in the lamentation and grief.

19. - CONCERNING THE LAMENTING
OF THE POOR LADIES AND HOW
THEY SOUGHT TO HAVE HIS BODY

1. How great was the grief of everyone; and, how intense the lamenting especially of the Poor Ladies! Being of womanly spirit, they could not at all control their weeping, but, sighing from the depths of their hearts, they shed inconsolable tears. 2. They sighed, «Woe to us, most benign father! Why did death, the mother of sorrow, spare us for a time if not to torment us more cruelly by irrevocably taking you away? 3. Our poverty was enough for us to make us count as riches the fact that we could hear at least in some manner what he, whom we did not merit to see with our bodily eyes, was preaching to others, namely, the word of life.»

4. While they were loudly bewailing these and other things, there were some among them who said, «Why are we throwing to the wind all these tears and sighs filled with sobbing, as if we could accompany with grief a dead person who has become immortal and whose presence the angels, his fellow citizens, now enjoy? 5. There is only one remedy for this painful separation: the one who in life was not allowed to show us his bodily presence should remain with us at least after death.»

6. Some asked, «But how can this be done?

We are sure that the friars who live in the southern part of the city will not allow that the most holy body of Anthony remain with us unless perhaps they are influenced by the petitions of more important people to cede their right out of merciful kindness. 7. Let us then send some people who will approach on behalf of our petitions the authoritative persons of the city, both religious and nobles with secular power, so that they all work together, but as if we were not involved, in order to have with the friars' consent what we ask for devoutly.»

8. And this was done. Why say more? All of them assented by unanimous agreement to the wishes of Christ's handmaidens and promised to offer their help without question.

20. - HOW THE INHABITANTS OF CAPO DI PONTE OPPOSED THE FRIARS WHO PLANNED TO TAKE HIS BODY TO THEIR CHURCH

1. The friars who lived at the Church of the Holy Mother of God, [4] having come to Arcella, made plans to transfer the revered body of blessed Anthony to their own place. They considered it a most unworthy and intolerable evil to be deprived of so great a treasure, especially because the saint himself, when he was still alive, preferred that convent much more than any other in the province. He liked the place so much that, when he felt his death approaching, he commanded under obedience the friar who was assisting him to take all care that his body be carried to the Church the Holy Mother of

---

[4] The present Basilica of St. Anthony stands at that spot.

God.[5]   3. Hearing this, the inhabitants of Capo di Ponte unanimously opposed the friars to their faces and, so that what the friars intended could not in any way be done, increased the armed guards and ordered that the place be watched day and night.

4. Not knowing what to do, the friars hastily went to the bishop of the city and presented their whole preoccupation to this father of orphans.   5. When he had called together his confreres, the canons, to obtain their advice, he diligently set out the friars' reason for coming there and asked each one's opinion concerning the case.   6. Some of them, influenced beforehand by the entreaties of the Poor Ladies, considered the friars' petition not to have any value at all. What is more, introducing their own reasons into the matter, they argued even more forcefully in favour of the Poor Ladies.

7. But no less did the friars know how to use what supported their own case, insisting on the conditions of the dead person and on the fact itself, and, with reasons that were not unimportant, they exerted themselves to persuade the bishop to decide il their favour.   8. The bishop, therefore, judging the friars petition to be reasonable, consented to all their desires and ordered the magistrate of the city[6] to offer them assistance.

21. - CONCERNING THE PEOPLE'S DEVOTION AND A MIRACLE FROM HEAVEN

1. In the meantime, while these matters were being debated, a group of people from Capo di

---

[5] Inasmuch as Anthony was a member of this community or convent, he had the right to be buried in its church.

[6] The city magistrate was Stephen Badoer, a Venetian nobleman.

Ponte grew more vehement in wanting the body of blessed Anthony and, denying access to the magistrate, their minds became more obstinate against every prohibition. 2. A meeting of the elders was held and of all those who could be trusted to give some advice, and friends were called from the city so that they could help. 3. In short, they all reached the point that they swore an oath that their persons, possessions and whatever else they owned would be put in jeopardy before they allowed the body of the most blessed Anthony even to be moved from its place.

4. What I narrate is truly extraordinary. Zeal and devout fervour had so made all their wills collaborate towards the one goal that, although some of them had lived for a long time in disharmony because of inveterate hatred and internal city conflicts, now, having forgotten, as it seemed, the old enmities, they agreed unanimously and amicably in their sole purpose of keeping the body of blessed Anthony. 5. Fearing, therefore, lest they be frustrated in their hope by some deceitful scheme and having taken counsel among themselves, they decided to carry away the body.

6. Indeed, since the minister provincial was not present, and the friars' cause depended on his consent, after having called apart their elders, they began to beg the friars that they at least wait some time for the provincial's arrival and, in the meantime, desist from their plan so that everything be left completely to his decision. 7. What they said was acceptable, for the general opinion of all the citizens agreed with it.

8. When, therefore, nighttime fell and the crowds were made to leave, the friars closed the

doors of the house and reinforced them with bars and bolts so as to prevent a possible raid by the people. 9. Towards midnight, however, while the guards were still keeping watch, an excited crowd of people, aflame with desire to see the body, impudently broke down all the bars, together with the doors, and violently rushed against the house where the holy body was lying. 10. Having already repeated this same attack three times, they provoked the friars but—strange to say—could not, despite their efforts, enter the house even once. But, as they themselves later confessed, when the doors were opened, they suddenly stood senseless and, since the house was filled with light and they could not see the entrance, they ran around as if charmed by the brilliance.

11. In the morning, then, many faithful people from the city, villages and castles came to see the most blessed body of Anthony. Whoever could at least once touch it in some way considered himself truly fortunate. 12. Those, on the other hand, who could not draw close enough because of the crowd, would throw at random through the windows and doors their embroidered girdles and money-belts, rings and necklaces, keys and other ornaments. Still others, attaching these same articles to long poles, would reach within so that they might have them back, sanctified by contact with the most revered body.

22. - CONCERNING THE PEOPLE'S RESTLESSNESS AND THE MINISTER'S ARRIVAL

1. Since the minister was tardy in arriving and because it was summer, a time that is unkind to the burial of bodies, the friars quickly (as best as possible to those who are disturbed) enclosed his remains in a wooden coffin and buried them in a shallow grave, hoping to find a better site later. 2. This was hardly done, when a voice was suddenly heard of someone saying, «The body has been carried away!»

3. The people, hearing this and quickly having become restless, assaulted the house of the friars with swords and clubs, and, having violently thrown to the ground barricades and doors, ran together to the place where the holy body lay buried. And they did not desist from their intent until—what shall I say, moved by frenzy or more likely by spiritual fervor?—digging in the ground, they found the coffin in which the precious treasure was hidden. 4. And, having found that precious pearl, they would not believe the friars who insisted that the body was inside the ark but, instead, by hitting the top with a stake, they were assured that it was so by the muffled sound.

5. Saturday evening, the minister provincial came, whose return the whole city was anxiously awaiting. 6. When the inhabitants of Capo di Ponte saw him, they quickly convoked their council and insistently asked for the body of blessed Anthony. In favour of their cause, they adduced far-fetched arguments, and, so that the friars might at least give in out of fear, they accompanied those arguments with threats. 7. In the end, they brought forth the document in which they had written their pact, de-

claring clearly to all, that, in defence of their cause, they would not yield to irons, swords, or even death, and that, as long as they lived, they would never fall short of what they had agreed upon.

8. To which, the minister replied, «My very dear people, by right, you cannot ask anything of what you are trying so excitedly to demonstrate. On the other hand, if you are talking of benevolent kindness, then, with our friars' advice, we will actively pursue what the Lord inspires. 9. Nevertheless, for the love of peace and so that I will not seem to have spoken to you deceitfully—you should fear that deplorable suspicion—I concede that you guard the place where the body of blessed Anthony rests, unless, with the deliberation of the friars, we dispose otherwise about the things you seek.»

23. - CONCERNING THE DECISION IN FAVOR
OF THE FRIARS AND ABOUT THE
DESTRUCTION OF THE BRIDGE

1. It was already the third day. Seeing that it would be difficult for him to resist alone the will of so many and of that kind of people, especially because the matter touched them all, the minister went to the city magistrate and, when the urban council was convoked, humbly asked them for advice and help. 2. With the consent of all, the city magistrate ordered that the place where the sacred body lay be guarded and, lest anyone do violence to the friars, forbade, under a fine of one hundred pounds, that anyone carry arms to the place, until it be known what had been legally established by the bishop and clergy of the city, to whom the decision belonged.

3. On the fourth day after the death of blessed Anthony, therefore, having convoked the clergy of the city, the bishop entered into council with them and began loyally and sincerely to discuss how the peace among the inhabitants was to be preserved and how the friars' right was to be safeguarded. 4. Having asked respectively the opinion of the elders and the learned, he began to debate on the merits of the case; but, as we already stated above, he discovered that the more influential among them were previously swayed by the entreaties of the Poor Ladies and leaned in their favour.

5. The minister, then, rising from the midst of the friars and asking for silence with his hand, spoke out, «As I see it, to save the peace of the more influential, they, who place on both dishes of the scales of justice only the total weight of affection and nothing of right reason, do not quite equally weigh righteousness and benevolence. I admit that they are moved by divine zeal, but not wisely. 6. Anthony was a friar of our order and, unless they want to ignore it, although they saw it with their own eyes, he always remained with us. Therefore, we are asking for one who entrusted himself to us and who, while he was still alive, we know had chosen over all others the Church of the Holy Mother of God for his burial place. 7. If, by chance, you contend that he could not choose his place of burial because his will was tied by bonds of saving obedience, then, we ask: To whom do you think is reserved this authority and freedom of choice, if not to his superior? 8. We, although unworthy, who exercise the office of superior, therefore, humbly ask to be given what by recognized right and evident reason is owed to us.»

9. The bishop, when he heard the reasons of both parties, established with his definitive decision that from that moment on everything was to be done according to the minister's will and whatever had been said or done was to be submitted to his judgment in order to be either invalidated or confirmed. 10. Then, he commanded his clergy that the next day, the fifth after the death of blessed Anthony, they prepare themselves as usual and gather early in the morning at Arcella in orderly procession. 11. He also ordered the city magistrate to offer help to the friars and to hasten, with prepared groups of people, to Arcella at the appointed time to transport the body of blessed Anthony.

12. The magistrate, obligingly accepted his directive, consented and ordered that as soon as possible a bridge of boats and wooden planks be built across the river which flowed through Arcella. Indeed, he was afraid that, if the procession passed through the center of Capo di Ponte, the people's indignation would stir up a rebellion. 13. As soon as it was built, however, the devout people of Capo di Ponte, spiritually fervent but furious with indignation at the construction of the bridge, ran to the spot with axes and swords and, in their bold recklessness, reduced it to pieces. 14. Indeed, there you would have seen the contorted frenzy as of a woman in the pains of labour and heard furious shouting while they destroyed with axes the boats in the water as if cutting wood in a forest.

15. Why say more? The whole city was stirred up, especially because the crime brought harm to the common good. 16. And while they were still shouting, it was learned that the people who lived in

the southern part of the city were coming armed, hand in hand. 17. Hearing this, the inhabitants of Capo di Ponte took a position facing them, drawn up in fighting formations and ready for battle if the approaching group were but to touch their houses or carry away the body of blessed Anthony to some other place.

24. - CONCERNING THE FRIARS' WEEPING AND THE TRANSFERAL OF BLESSED ANTHONY'S BODY

1. Seeing that the complete ruin of the city was imminent, the friars were overcome by great dread and, through their sad weeping and tears, kept saying, «Woe to us! This storm has arisen because of us, and, unless the Lord protects it, almost the whole city will be destroyed on our account. 3. How shall we go on living if so many thousands of men perish in the defence of our cause? 4. Hear us, Lord; reconcile us, Lord; turn to us and intervene! Why do you hide your face, and, totally forgetting, not show mercy for this affliction of ours? 5. We wanted peace and it did not come; we looked for what was good, and behold disaster. 6. For your own self, O Lord, our God, hear and answer your children; do not let this city be destroyed.»

7. In the same way, having heard what was about to take place, the venerable handmaidens of Christ began to lament and, blaming themselves for what might occur, they asked with increased prayers and abundant tears that the holy body be taken away which they formerly begged with all desire to be given. Everyone—men and women of whatever age and condition—awaited God's merciful kind-

ness with an anxious heart.

9. And, since he does not forget to be merciful, God came to their aid at the right moment. Indeed, the One who does not fail to show his providential care allowed for the increase of his greater glory that the people be disturbed for some time so that he might bring to a more wonderful end what he was planning to do. 10. The One who is eternally good does not permit evil in society unless he can at the same time draw out what is useful to the profit of those who are good. 11. The city magistrate, who could not tolerate the people's insurrection, called all the inhabitants to the palace through a proclamation of the town crier. When the council had been gathered, he confined to the southern part of the city those who had destroyed the bridge and forbade by edict, under oath and threat of confiscation of all their goods, that they return to their homes that day.

12. Later, the bishop of the city with all the clergy and the magistrate with a swollen number of inhabitants came to Arcella. When the funeral cortege was formed, amid hymns, praises and spiritual canticles, and accompanied by the extraordinary exultation of all people, they transported the body of most blessed Anthony through the centre of Capo di Ponte to the Church of Mary, the Holy Mother of God. .13. The nobles among the people and the leading citizens of the city carried the bier on their shoulders, and those who could but lightly touch it considered themselves fortunate.

14. So great was the onrush of people that, because of the multitudes, many could not move at once through the centre of the city. Thus, wandering through the squares, narrow streets and the

outskirts of the city, they quickly overtook the funeral procession. 15. They all brought as many candles as they could procure, and such was the abundance of these lights that the whole city glowed as if set ablaze by fire.

16. When the procession reached the Church of Mary, the Holy Mother of God, the bishop, having solemnly celebrated Mass buried the body of blessed Anthony in an honourable manner, and, when he had terminated the funeral rites, he returned to his residence amid the exultation of all those present.

25. - CONCERNING THE MIRACLES GENERALLY GRANTED THAT VERY DAY

1. That same day, there were carried to the tomb of the saint very many people suffering from various illnesses, and immediately they were cured and restored to their original health through the merits of blessed Anthony. 2. In fact, whoever was ill and touched the ark, as soon as he was let down, felt freed from whatever malady afflicted him. 3. And those who could not remain before the ark, because of the multitude of the sick who came there, and, therefore, stayed outside the door of the church, regained their health in the square in full view of all the people.

4. There, indeed, the eyes of the blind were opened; the ears of the deaf, unblocked. There, the limping jumped like deer; the loosed tongues of the mute quickly and clearly acclaimed God. 5. There, paralyzed limbs reacquired their original use; deformities, gout, fever or any other maladies were miraculously put to flight. 6. There, indeed, all de-

sired benefits were granted to the faithful; there, those who came from different parts of the world, both men and women obtained the healing they requested.

26. - CONCERNING PROCESSIONS
AND THE PEOPLE'S DEVOTION

1. The devotion of the people was aroused through the most clearly radiant light of the miracles, and the gathering of the dispersed people of Israel was symbolized by God's construction of a new Jerusalem. 2. And, truly, from east to west, from north and south, people came in well-ordered procession. Seeing the marvellous signs which happened before their eyes through the merits of blessed Anthony, they extolled with due honour the virtues of his holy life.

3. As we said, among those who came in ordered processions to offer devoutly their homage of praise to God and to his blessed servant Anthony, the first to come were the inhabitants of Capo di Ponte, precisely they who had, because of their strong passion, reduced to pieces the bridge so that the holy body might not be taken away from them. 4. Truly, shedding tears and walking barefoot, and preceded by the clergy with crosses and banners, they all came to the sepulchre of blessed Anthony with reverence which was so extraordinary to everyone as to rend the hearts of the faithful who looked on, moving them to compunction and inviting them to the fire of divine love.

5. Indeed, even if it were made of iron, whose breast would not be moved to tears and not be strengthened with good intentions at the sight of

knights—a delicate sort of people—walking along difficult roads, and noble women, who could hardly hold themselves up because of the softness of their lives, following barefoot the steps of those who preceded them? 6. Imitating their extraordinary devotion, especially since in the cause to possess the saint's body they were zealous adversaries, and to bring about more fruitful peace of the heart, the friars went out in procession to honour them, singing hymns in chorus.

7. Not only these but the whole population of the city, grouped according to its districts, came on established days, walking barefoot in procession. Religious, of whom the city has many, also came in procession and barefoot, accompanying the inhabitants of the districts where they lived. 8. In his own turn, the bishop with the holy gathering of his clergy approached the tomb, reverently and barefoot. And the city magistrate, coming with groups of knights and large crowds of people, took off his footwear.

9. Similarly the holy communities of religious who lived in great numbers in the villages and castles of the surrounding region, having put on sacred vestments, ran barefoot with joyous devotion along the difficult roads. 10. Then, came the crowd of students, of whom there is a large number in the city of Padua.[7] And, mixing songs with sad hymns, they recalled the sighs mixed with joy of those children who returned to rebuild the temple of God. A mourner would sing a hymn and, in the midst of his lament, would break out in jubilation.

---

[7] The University of Padua began when a large group of professors and students abandoned the University of Bologna in 1222.

11. Thus, precisely thus, the well-ordered groups—what shall I say: of those who sang joyously and of those who cried—came barefoot, preceded by a candle of such great size that, unless its greater part had not been cut off, it could not have been set up straight under the roof of the Church of the Holy Mother of God.[8]   12. Not only students but also other groups of people, who came on their appointed day, brought candles of such height that most, unless they were broken off, could not be introduced into the church.

13. Such extraordinary candles were carried on shoulders that sixteen bent men hardly sufficed to support one; or, if the candles were brought by carts, then two pairs of bulls, yoked together, would be attached to pull them.   14. These were very high candles. From their extended limbs on both sides—as in the lampstand—there came out spheres and lilies, vines and various types of flowers, all accurately fashioned by the hand of an artist.

15. Some had the form of a religious building; others, the terrible battle of an army.   16. Furthermore, some who had adorned the procession with such a wonderful gift of candles also carried lit candles by hand.   17. And, when they could not draw close to the entrance of the church because of the crowd, in confusion they would pile up the tapers and candles in the square before the door of the temple.

18. Some, arranging their lamps above walls, would keep watch during the night in the squares.

---

[8] The church must have been quite small and low, and, since its roof was probably made of wood, it had to be protected from the flames of long candles.

And it was something truly marvellous because they neither yielded to the heat of summer nor gave up because of the sluggish cold of winter, but, with invincible spirits in their breasts, continuing day and night, and taking turns, they spent every moment of time praising God.

19. The city rejoiced to be adorned with such great splendours and, brightened by so many lights, it seemed to have lost all its nightly darkness. 20. Venetians came running; the people of Treviso hurried; there could be seen inhabitants from Vicenza, Lombards, Slavs, people from Aquileia, Germans, Hungarians. All of them, seeing with the eyes of faith that signs were renewed and marvels multiplied, were praising and glorifying the Creator's omnipotence.

21. All those, who came and saw with their eyes and touched with their hands the extraordinary things that were certainly being performed through the merits of blessed Anthony, were filled with confidence that they would receive the grace they desired, and they confessed their sins to the friars, who were hardly sufficient for so great a number. 22. Moreover, those who came looking for a cure and, according to what is written, hid their sins in secret, could not be guided onto the path of health. But, if they confessed and at last abandoned for their own good their evil ways, then they felt merciful healing, immediately and in the sight of all.

27. - CONCERNING THE DELEGATE'S MISSION TO THE CURIA FOR ST. ANTHONY'S CANONIZATION

1. The faith of the Church came to be exalted; highest poverty was esteemed and simple humility

was honoured. Faithlessness, the blind mother of error, was put to shame, and the mind made foolish by heretical wickedness languished in pallid decay. Indeed, diffident impiety was confused and the darkness of unbelief was dissipated by the splendours of miracles, as if by the rising of a new light.

2. Truly, the holy assembly of the clergy called for it; the devout people loudly cried for it; all agreed with one voice and unanimous desire, and insisted with every wish, that delegates be sent to the curia for blessed Anthony's canonization. 3. Accordingly, a solemn assembly of clergy and lay people was organized to discuss this matter, and it was decided in plenary council that the unanimous desire of the multitude be heeded. 4. Why say more? The bishop with the clergy wrote a petition; the city magistrate with the nobles and people did so too. Not even a month after the saint's death, they sent delegates, known for the seriousness of their virtues and respected for their states in life, to the Apostolic See.

5. Some days later, when they presented themselves in the sight of the pope and diligently set out the reasons for their coming, the delegates were received most agreeably by Pope Gregory IX and by all those present in the curia, 6. although many of them were rather astonished by what they heard about the sudden glory of the man of God and the unexpectedness of his many miracles. 7. The sacred college of cardinals was therefore convoked and a solemn reunion was held concerning the cause of the Paduan representatives. 8. At last, with the general advice of all, the examination of the miracles was entrusted by the supreme pontiff to the venerable bishop of Padua and to the priors

of St. Benedict [9] and of the Friars Preachers.

9. Not insignificant crowds of both men and women ran from everywhere to Padua, in order to affirm with proof of truth that they were freed from various misfortunes through the glorious merits of blessed Anthony. Thereupon, an extremely large number of miracles came to light. 10. A hearing was given to testimonies which were confirmed under oath, and, having gathered many trustworthy witnesses, the reports of approved miracles were set down in writing. 11. Indeed, for the greater confirmation of faith and miracles, the conditions of the persons and of the fact were scrupulously investigated; place and time, what was seen and heard, and if any other circumstances were pertinent to the testimonies, were all carefully written down.

12. When the examination of the miracles was therefore diligently completed, the faithful people of Padua continued to insist with vigorous devotion, and, after the second and third groups of representatives, chose delegates worthy of trust to be sent to the Apostolic See. 13. In fact, to inform the pope who was solicitous and the cardinals who were watchful about the truthfulness of the case and the worthiness of the devotion, the venerable bishop of Padua sent to the curia friars and canons of the principal church, accompanied by the prior of the Church of Saint Mary at Montecroce; the city magistrate, on the other hand, sent nobles and those who were powerful, counts and knights, with a large group of illustrious persons and a crowd of people. 14. In the same manner, the whole univer-

---

[9] The reference is to Blessed Jordan Forzaté, prior of the monastery of St. Benedict in Padua.

sity—professors and students—wrote a letter worthy of consideration; and the guild of writers sent a letter which could not be lightly dismissed, offering a testimony of what was seen and heard.

15. The venerable cardinals who were present—through the Lord's intervention—also wrote about all these things. Indeed, at that time, Lord Oddo of Monferrato and Lord James, bishop-elect of Palestrina, were busy as papal legates in reestablishing peace among some cities in Lombardy and in the March of Treviso. 16. When, on the occasion of the said legation, they came to Padua and learned through eyewitnesses and with most certain truth of the marvellous deeds of the Lord, they themselves, becoming witnesses to the truth, confirmed the credibility of the miracles with the support of their own letter.

17. Having taken these letters, the delegates quickly reached the curia, and, supported by so many and such influential documents, they were most kindly received by the lord pope and by his whole court. 18. Why say anything more? Again an assembly was gathered and the canonization of most blessed Anthony was quite favourably discussed in the presence of the lord pope and of all the cardinals. At last, convoking a consistory, a general examination of the miracles and the approval of those examined was entrusted to Lord John, bishop of Sabina. [10] 19. Now, that lord by no means acted phlegmatically in the office entrusted to him, but promoted the cause quite solicitously, and thor-

---

[10] The archbishop of Besançon became the cardinal of Sabina in 1227. In 1230, he was involved in reconciling Emperor Frederick II and Pope Gregory IX.

oughly completed the examination and approval within a space of time that no one expected.

28. - CONCERNING A VISION GIVEN FROM HEAVEN

1. During the discussion of these matters, behold a new and unforeseen difficulty became urgent for the Paduan delegates. The joy of the preceding results was disturbed by a point that was raised. 2. There were certain cardinals who, by reason of their virtues and learning, stood out among the other princes of the Church. These, because of their zeal for ecclesiastical custom and because they were worried by the short time that had elapsed, judged that it was not necessary to act so precipitately in such an important case, especially because not even a year had gone by since blessed Anthony's death. Therefore, they prudently asserted that they neither could nor wished to consent to his canonization unless the due limit of time had passed.

3. But the One, who testifies through the voice of the prophet that he does not give his glory to another, willed that the case be stopped for the time of those words so that it be acknowledged that the whole completion of our works must be attributed to his grace. 4. And, at the opportune time, he intervened mercifully and through a vision, miraculously persuaded one of those cardinals in favour of the canonization.

5. This was the mental vision he had. As he slept, he saw the lord pope dressed in pontifical robes, standing ready to consecrate a church and an altar. The venerable cardinals, who served him as usual in the sacred rites, formed a kind of crown around him. Among them, not last in office or dig-

nity, and dressed in sacred vestments, the sleeper stood ready to serve. 6. When the moment for the consecration approached, the supreme pontiff asked for the relics that were to be placed, according to the ritual, within the altar, but they, one by one, answered that they didn't have any. 7. Then, the pope, looking around searchingly, saw by chance a recently dead body wrapped in cloths, lying close by. As soon as he saw it, he said, «Quickly bring me these new relics to place within the altar.»

8. But the cardinals, when they saw the body, immediately insisted that it was not a relic. Then the pope said, «Remove the cloth with which it is covered and at least look at what lies within.» 9. Moving with slow steps and unwillingly, they drew close to the body, and, carrying out the order, swiftly removed the cloth in which it was wrapped. 10. But, when they had uncovered it and did not smell even the least odour then, turning towards the body, they were so bleased with the relic that they tried to outdo each other in contending who would come to own it.

11. At the pushing of those who rushed to the body, all of which he saw in the dream, the cardinal was shocked out of his sleep and shortly rose from his bed. Having called to himself the clerics who served him, he immediately described the dream and devoutly gave its interpretation by referring it to the canonization of blessed Anthony, stating that, without any doubt, it would soon take place. 12. While he was coming down from his quarters to go to the curia, behold the Paduan delegates, as if led by divine beckoning, stood at the door. 13. As soon as he saw them, the cardinal turned to the clerics who waited on him and, with a cheerful look

on his face, said, «Behold our dream and its interpretation!»

14. Comforted, therefore, by the divine vision, he became so great a promoter of the Paduans' cause as to argue firmly that God's omnipotence could not be limited by time and the saint's glory ought not to be impeded by any custom.

29. - CONCERNING THE SAINT'S CANONIZATION

1. As was mentioned above, when the reports of the miracles were read publicly before Lord John, the bishop of Sabina, and when they were verified and attested by sworn notaries, declared approved and accepted, then all the cardinals and prelates who were at the time present in the curia gathered together. 2. At last, the motion in favour of blessed Anthony's canonization was made and, since all agreed on it, the reunion was celebrated with great joy.

3. «It would be totally unworthy—let it never happen!—that we impede on earth the veneration due to the merits of the most blessed father Anthony whom the Lord of majesty deigned to crown in heaven with glory and honour. 4. Indeed, just as it would be false not to believe the truth of miracles that have been confirmed, so also to deny the praise due to the merits of saints would amount to a kind of envy.» 5. At last, seeing that all unanimously consented to saint Anthony's canonization and keeping in mind no less the indefatigable devotion of the people of Padua, the supreme pontiff, with the general advice of all, assented to their suppliant petition and, setting aside every delay, fixed the day when it was to be celebrated.

6. It was already the third day appointed for so great a solemnity. The sacred college of cardinals was present, bishops were convoked, abbots came, and prelates of churches from various parts of the world came running. On one side was gathered the holy assembly of the clergy; on the other, a multitude of people that could hardly be counted. 7. The supreme pontiff stood upright in magnificent glory, dressed in pontifical robes; and, the college of cardinals and other princes of the Church, all dressed in sacred vestments, gathered around the anointed of the Lord. 8. At last, the reports of the miracles were read as usual before all the people, and the glorious merits of blessed father Anthony were extolled with highest devotion and reverence.

9. Filled with holy consolation and as he stood, the shepherd of the Church raised his arms to heaven and, having invoked the name of the most holy Trinity, enrolled the most blessed father Anthony in the catalogue of saints and ordered that his feast be celebrated on the day of his death—to the praise and glory of the Father, and the Son and the Holy Spirit, to whom be all honour and power for ever and ever. Amen.

10. All of this took place in the city of Spoleto, in the year of Our Lord 1232, in the fifth indiction, on the day of Pentecost, [11] in the sixth year of the pontificate of the Lord Pope Gregory IX.

11. Thus, quickly hurrying home, the delegates of the city of Padua returned to joyous feasting, all of this having taken place before the end of the first year after blessed Anthony's death. And they cele-

---

[11] That year, Pentecost was celebrated on May 30.

brated his feast with indescribable solemnity that very day, a year after his departure for heaven.

HERE BEGIN THE MIRACLES
OF BLESSED ANTHONY

30. - PROLOGUE

1. To the praise and glory of almighty God, Father and Son and Holy Spirit, of the glorious Virgin Mary and of St. Anthony, and in order to animate the devotion of the faithful, we are led to write briefly but with full truth about the miracles which were read in the presence of the Lord Pope Gregory and in the listening of all the people.

31. - CONCERNING THE PHYSICALLY DISABLED

1. (I) The day when the body of the most blessed Anthony was buried with honour in the Church of Mary, the Holy Mother of God, a certain woman by the name of Cunizza who had been seriously ill a for year, supporting herself on those wooden instruments which people call crutches, was able to come up to the place. 2. On her shoulder, caused by a congealing of fluids, a monstrous hump had developed and so miserably bent her low that, without the support of crutches, she could not walk at all. 3. When she had briefly remained prostrate in prayer before the tomb of the most blessed Antho-

ny, her shoulder rapidly straightened out, the hump disappeared and, setting aside the crutches, the woman, made upright again, returned home.

4. (II) A certain woman, by the name of Guilla, for eight years and more had been so bent over, because her left shin was dried up and her nerves drawn in, that she could not at all put her foot on the ground. But, when out of necessity she wanted to move somewhere, she would drag her body with difficulty, supporting herself on crutches. 5. Her husband, Marcoardo, having placed her on a horse, quickly brought her to the Church of Mary, the Holy Mother of God, and, when he got her inside, he devoutly found a spot for her before blessed Anthony's ark so that she might regain her health. 6. Lying prostrate in prayer, she immediately began to feel such great pain that, perspiring because of her anguish, she could not bear the heat. With the help of men, she was taken outside the church and, breathing the fresh air, she again felt better. 7. Shortly after, she was led back to the tomb. While she was praying with closed eyes, she felt as if a hand had touched her stomach and had tried to raise her body. 8. Wanting to know who it was who touched her, she opened her eyes but did not see anyone near to her. 9. When the woman therefore understood that what she had felt was divine aid, she rose immediately and, throwing aside her crutches, joyfully returned home with her husband.

10. (III) Another woman, whose name was Riccarda, for twenty years suffered from legs that were atrophied. She had become so monstrously drawn in by a certain calloused joining of the skin

that her knees stuck to her chest and her feet to her buttocks. One day, using crutches instead of her feet, she came with certain paupers to the place of blessed father Anthony to receive alms from passersby. 11. When, overcome by drowsiness, she fell asleep with her head slightly bent toward the ground, she heard a voice, saying, «Thanks be to God because she is freed!» 12. When she opened her eyes, she saw a girl who was hunchbacked but had been made whole again through the merits of the most saintly father. The girl was leaving with many people accompanying her. 13. The woman therefore got up as best she could so that she too might come to the tomb to be cured. While she was making her way there, behold a seven-year-old boy appeared to her and, preceding her with closed hands, invited her to enter, saying, «Come in the name of the Lord because he will free you.» 14. Following the footsteps of the youngster, she dragged herself as usual on crutches up to the door of the church, but, when she reached the threshold of the door, the boy disappeared. 15 Entering the place of the sepulchre, she wholly devoted herself to prayer. While she was thus praying, behold two round balls like eggs broke out between her shin and flank. Running within a kind of fluid under her skin, the balls descended all the way to her feet, making a noise like the sound of clapping hands, a sound that was heard by many. 16. At last, her legs which had been made dry like wood for twenty years immediately gained in length, and, the skin having stretched itself, the flesh began to grow to its original size. 17. When the custodians at the tomb saw what was happening, they very hastily carried the woman outside the door of the church and sent her away, not at all fully healed. 18. But she, insisting in prayer for nineteen days and daily dragging herself to the same spot, finally, on the twentieth day threw away her crutches and returned home, walking through the centre of the city with a firm pace, not without everyone's admiration.

19. (IV) A certain boy, whose name was Albert, from his birth until the age of eleven had a crooked left foot. Its upper part was turned downward and its toes were reversed toward the heal of the right foot. 20. His father, in order to straighten out the foot, would often bind it to wooden splints. But, whenever it was unbound, it would immediately spring back into its usual contortion. 21. On a certain day, therefore, the boy's mother suppliantly came with him to blessed Anthony's ark and somehow got his foot to touch it. Although he remained there for a short time, the boy nevertheless perspired greatly. When he was given back to his mother by the custodians at the ark, he returned home with the soles of his feet set properly on the ground.

22. (V) A certain girl, called Agnes, for almost three years was without any bodily strength.[1] She was suffering so much from the sickness which people call anatropy that she languished dehydrated like a piece of dry wood. 23. As soon as she took any food, she would immediately throw it up, ripe and wholly undigested. The malady had already advanced so much that, her throat being blocked by excessive dehydration, she could hardly swallow sa-

---

[1] Her general bodily disfunctions provoked frequent vomiting.

liva or even anything mild. 24. When doctors would come to restrain her continual vomiting and to restore her natural fluid balance with the benefit of their art, not being able to do anything and despairing of her health, they would leave. 25. One day, therefore, she was taken to the church and placed in prayer above blessed Anthony's ark. Suddenly gripped by extreme pain throughout her body, she seemed to be close to dying. 26. When the pain which had attacked her subsided a little, she called to her mother, who was standing close to the place, saying that now she could swallow a whole loaf of bread. At last, having taken her daughter with herself, the mother returned home and, immediately able to retain food, the girl's dehydrated body regained its original health.

27. (VI) In the city of Venice, a certain woman called Cesaria had a shortened hand and, for more than two years, walked with a left foot that was curved sideways. 28. When she came to the diocese of Padua at harvest time to gather, as is the custom of poor people, the grain which escaped the hands of reapers, and heard what was happening through the merits of blessed Anthony, she came, not without great difficulty, to the city of Padua in the hope of recovering her health. 29. Since she could not draw close to the ark because of the large number of sick people, she tried to touch the place of the sepulchre by pushing her leg through the stakes[2] which surrounded the ark. 30. When, with her leg stretched out, she extended the foot and

---

[2] These stakes probably formed a kind of fence to hold back anyone who yielded to uncontrollable forms of devotion.

touched the ark, so great a pain seized her immediately that she perspired greatly out of distress, her innermost parts being shaken deeply as if threatening to break out. 31. Those who were present, when they saw the woman's suffering, for she could not speak because of her weak condition, carried her close to the wall of the church so that she could find rest. 32. When she stayed there for a little while, her perspiration stopped and she suddenly stood up. Having been healed in hand and foot, she departed thanking God.

33. (VII) Prosdocima of Noventa, the widow of Mainerio, had a left hand and both feet that were contracted. She was carried to blessed Anthony's sepulchre in a wooden tub. 34. When she was raised above the ark, her feet were immediately straightened out and restored to their original use through the merits of blessed Anthony. Her hand, to be sure, opened a little, trembling at first, and then stretched out so that, while everyone looked on, she closed and opened it. 35. Taken down from the ark, she at once jumped to her feet and, having regained the health she desired, she departed full of joy.

36. (VIII) A certain inhabitant of Padua, called Peter, had a daughter whose name was Padovana. Although she was four years old, she was absolutely incapable of using her feet and moved like a reptile, crawling with the help of her hands. Furthermore, it was said that, since she suffered from epilepsy, she would often fall and roll around. 37. When saint Anthony was still alive, her father, as he carried her in his arms while walking through

the city one day, met the saint and began to beg him to make the sign of the cross over his daughter. 38. The saintly father, admiring the man's faith, blessed her and sent her away. When the girl's father returned home, he made his daughter stand up on her feet. Supported by a footstool, she immediately began to walk about. 39. Then, having taken away the footstool, her father gave her a cane. Indeed, walking about in the house, the girl always improved. 40. At last, through the merits of most blessed Anthony, she healed completely and did not need any prop whatsoever. And, from that moment when she was blessed, she no longer suffered any illness or even the least falling sickness.

41. (IX) A certain woman, whose name was Mary, when she was once watching her father's mares along the river Brenta, sat alone under a certain nut tree. Behold a black man walked out of the river, came straight towards her, took her into his arms, and carried her to another nut tree which was close by. 42. Wanting to do her violence, he threw her, frightened as she was, to the ground and left her so badly fractured that, with a hump on her chest, a knee drawn in and a hipbone pulled out of her side, she returned home only with the help of her father. 43. She suffered this monstrous contraction for more than five years. 44. One night, however, after blessed Anthony's death, her knee and foot straightened out and she got up without any prop. Nevertheless, the hump on her chest and also the dislocated bone remained. 45. But, one day, when she was taken to the tomb of most blessed Anthony, she came back restored completely to health. As she was being healed, it seemed to her

that a man's hand was being lightly passed between her flesh and bones, and her limbs which previously hurt from severe pain seemed to be covered as if with a smooth ointment.

46. (X) Nascinguerra of Sacile had had a contracted right shin for two years and bore his foot in suspension. 47. One day, when he had come with the use of crutches to blessed Anthony's ark, he began to perspire violently, and, since he could not at all bear the great pain that took hold of him, he withdrew somewhat from the ark. 48. Those who were present ran up to him and stood him up, as he was trying to raise himself. Immediately, in the view of everyone, the nerves of his foot distended themselves. 49. Then, setting aside his crutches, he hastily returned home. The people of the whole neighbourhood ran to meet him and, shedding tears and ringing bells, gave thanks to God and blessed Anthony.

50. (XI) A certain woman from Saonara, whose name was Mary, had lost as of twelve years all use of her limbs on the right side from the waist down so that she could hardly drag her contracted body, and, this, only if supported by stays. One day, she was brought on a cart to the tomb of the saintly father Anthony. 51. Since she remained above the ark in prayer from the time she entered until almost midday, the custodians, who became weary, shouted that she get up. At the sound of their voices, the woman got up without any prop, and, setting aside her stays, returned home perfectly freed from her disability.

52. (XII) A certain individual from Porciglia, called Scotus, reached the place of the friars, carried on a man's back. His feet were in a state of putrefaction and swollen with inflamation caused by nodular gout. 53. Having confessed to and received penance from a friar, he hastily and suppliantly made himself be taken to saint Anthony's ark. When he stayed here a little, he was suddenly cured and returned to the friar with such speed that the latter, greatly surprised by the short time that had elapsed, made the healed man walk around in the cloister. 54. At last, thanking God and blessed Anthony in the sight of all, the one who had come there carried on another's back returned home on his own feet.

55. (XIII) In Codigoro, there was a girl called Samaritan. Once, when she went with other girls into her father's field to gather vegetables, her knees were suddenly contracted, and she could not return home but had to be carried back by the others. Thus, since the malady grew stronger, for three years she moved about by crawling with the help of her hands and—a sad spectacle to see—she used to drag herself along the ground in a sitting position. 56. One day, therefore, having made her confession, the girl came suppliantly with her mother to blessed Anthony's tomb, and, after a very short time, restored to her original health, she hastened home on her own feet. 57. When this was announced in the hearing of the people of Codigoro, they immediately came running at the ringing of bells and venerated the magnificence of God which was manifested in her.

58. (XIV) In the castle of Montagnana there lived a woman, called Guina, who as of two years had a disabled shoulder and right hand. She couldn't carry anything whatsoever on her shoulder nor even raise her hand to her mouth. 59. One day, having gone to blessed Anthony's tomb for a first and a second time, and not feeling any kind of relief in her shoulder and arm, she went up to a friar who devoted himself to the listening of confessions. 60. Having, therefore, made her confession, she came for a third time to the ark and prostrated herself in prayer. While she was praying, her humerus suddenly began to hurt with an acute pain and her shoulder bone, rattling like the cracking of nuts, sprang back into its original position. 61. As the woman rose, there and then, her arm shook. In the sight of all, she returned home freed from her disabilities.

62. (XV) When Margaret, who lived in Padua, was sleeping one night, it seemed to her that she fell to the ground from on high. Rising abruptly, the woman found that her neck was twisted back and, her nerves having been contracted, her left hand and foot were so bent that, the heel being suspended, she could hardly touch the ground with the tips of her toes. 63. But, one day, when she was raised above saint Anthony's tomb and remained there for a short while, her neck quickly straightened out and her head regained its normal position, her hand and foot were healed, and the woman came down, freed from her disabilities.

64. (XVI) Iacopino, the son of Albert, who had a contracted hand and foot, as he remained for

a short time in prayer above saint Anthony's ark, he suddenly perspired greatly, extended his hand and foot, and, in the sight of the custodians of the ark, went away healthy and praising God.

65. (XVII) In the city of Padua, there was a certain boy, called John, whose chin for four years adhered to his chest so much that he could not raise his head in any way but walked about stooped forward, with his head at an angle. 66. One day, when his mother brought him to blessed Anthony's tomb, there and then, the boy himself raised his head and, cured, went back with his mother. But a cavity appeared in his chest, in the very spot where his chin had stuck.

67. (XVIII) Frederick, a man from the village of Concordia, suffered harm to his kidneys when he fell from the church of Polcenigo, and couldn't walk any more without the support of crutches. 68. Having made a vow, he came devoutly to the tomb of the saintly father Anthony and immediately regained his health. He returned without his crutches.

69. (XIX) A woman, whose name was Gertrude, for four years had a contracted right foot so that she couldn't even take a step without crutches. 70. One night, when she was overcome with heavy drowsiness, she fell asleep under a nut tree. It seemed to her that a white-haired man stood before her—short of height, of dignified bearing, dressed in a green garment and covered with a scarlet cloak. He said to her, «Young lady, must you sleep here?» And, again, he continued, «Stretch out your foot!»

71. As she stretched out her foot, he took her by the hand, straightened out her nerves, and immediately disappeared. 72. As she awoke, she cried out, saying, «I thank you, saint Anthony, because you freed me!» Picking up her crutches, the cured woman returned home and, to the glory of God, told many listeners of this vision.

HERE ENDS THE PART
CONCERNING THE PHYSICALLY DISABLED

32. - CONCERNING PARALYTICS

1. (XX) In the town of Ferrara, there was a certain woman called Mary, who as of four years suffered from general paralysis of the body. Her head and limbs trembled. When, for whatever necessity, she wanted to go any place, she was very often forced to walk backwards or sideways. 2. One day, when she poured out her prayer before saint Anthony's tomb, her nerves immediately began to feel pain and distended themselves. The woman rose, stood firmly on her feet, and, clearly restored to health, returned home.

3. (XXI) Armerina of Vicenza lived paralyzed for five years. No matter what effort she made, she could not take firm steps, but, whenever she stood up, she would shake forward and backward with trembling movements. 4. When she came to blessed Anthony's ark, she prostrated herself in prayer and immediately merited to have her original health restored.

5. (XXII) When Maynard of Ronchi had already been suffering from paralysis for twenty days so that he could not use his feet in any way whatsoever nor open his mouth to eat, he was brought on a cart full of hay to the Prato della Valle. 6. When the cart which carried him reached the place, he was then brought on a man's back to blessed Anthony's tomb where he prayed. 7. Having finished his prayers, he quickly stood up and, opening his mouth, praised God and blessed Anthony. He returned home on his own feet.

8. (XXIII) A certain woman, whose name was Bilia, for three years suffering tremors in her whole body, came shakingly, straitened as she was, to the ark of the saintly father Anthony. While she persisted in prayer before the sepulchre, the tremor became stronger and she felt her temperature rise greatly. 9. Men and women cried, moved to compassion by her trembling and perspiration. But, when she was taken outside the door of the church so that she might breathe a little, her temperature came down and, having been cured, she left the place.

10. (XXIV) In the castle of Montagnana, there lived a woman whose name was Solagna. Paralyzed for a year and a month, sho vowed to come to the sepulchre of the saintly father Anthony so that she might regain her health. 11. One night, as she slept, lying in her bed, she was awakened when she heard a loud noise as if the foot of the bed had been struck. Calling to a person who was close by, she asked whether he had heard anything. 12. Although he answered that no noise whatsoever had

been made, the scared woman sat up in bed, and, putting on a robe, stayed awake to keep watch. 13. She had waited only briefly when the bed was struck again. Scared even more, she made the sign of the cross on her forehead as she asked, «Who touched the bed?» 14. Then she heard a voice, saying to her, «Make the sign boldly.» She asked, «Who are you, Lord?» He answered, «I am Anthony.» Speaking loudly, she said, «Set me free, saint Anthony!» He answered, «Behold, you are made whole.» 15. When morning came, the woman who had been made strong got out of bed. From then on, she didn't feel any illness whatsoever.

33. - CONCERNING THE BLIND

1. (XXV) A girl, called Auriema, who had lost her sight for a year and a half, was brought to blessed Anthony's ark so that she might be cured. 2. When she touched her eyes with the cloth that covered the ark, she suddenly opened her eyelids, having merited to see the skylight.

3. (XXVI) A certain friar of the Order of Friars Minor, Theodoric by name, who for two years was deprived of sight in his left eye, devoutly came from the borders of Puglia to the ark of the saintly father Anthony. 4. When he had stayed some time with the friars of Padua, he began to ask insistently for the grace of a cure. At last, when he obtained his much desired sight, he went away thanking God.

5. (XXVII) In the city of Treviso, there lived a certain man, called Zambono, who for more than six

years could not see anything at all from his left eye. 6. One day, therefore, when he came to saint Anthony's sepulchre and stayed above it for a short time, he suddenly regained his sight and joyfully returned home.

7. (XXVIII) Leonard of Conegliano, who as of three years had been totally blind in one eye, saw so poorly through the other that he could distinguish the people he knew from those he didn't only by their voices. When he devoutly came to the tomb of the reverend father Anthony, and remained prostrate for a short time before the ark, pouring out his prayers, he was given the sight of both eyes and returned home.

8. (XXIX) A certain Alexia, who for five years had been blind in both eyes and could not see the light, came to the saint's ark and immediately received the vision she had lost.

9. (XXX) Fiora of Gemma, who lived in Loreo, since she had been for seven years completely blind in her left eye, was taken to blessed Anthony's tomb. Perfectly cured, she returned home.

10. (XXXI) A certain German woman, whose name was Caroline, was brought to the sepulchre of the most saintly father because for seven years she had been deprived of sight in both eyes. When she stayed there for a short time in prayer, she regained her sight through heavenly aid and happily returned home, praising God.

1. (XXXII) In the city of Venice, there was a certain man whose name was Leonard. His ears had been blocked as of four years, and, hearing nothing at all, he became deaf. 2. When he suppliantly came one day to blessed Anthony's tomb, he immediately regained his desired hearing.

3. (XXXIII) Another man, called Menico, since he had been totally deaf for two years, came to the saint's ark and departed suddenly cured.

4. (XXXIV) Roland, popularly called the Bulgarian, deaf for twenty years because of a certain head ailment which continued to grow stronger, after he had poured out prayers before the saint's tomb, was restored to his original health through the merits of blessed Anthony, and returned home.

35. - CONCERNING THE MUTE

1. (XXXV) A certain Bartholomew from Piove di Sacco, mute from birth and suffering from total bodily paralysis as of fourteen years, would always toss in his bed of pain. When, at last, he was brought to the sepulchre of blessed father Anthony and his tongue was loosed, he praised the Lord. And, the one who came there, carried on another's back, returned home on his own feet.

2. (XXXVI) A woman, whose name was Michelotta, had been mute for eleven years and could not say anything at all. Furthermore, she was weak from total physical exhaustion. 3. Since she heard of the

miracles which were being performed through God's holy man, Anthony, she had herself carried to his tomb. After she had stayed there a little in sincere prayer, she departed, able to speak and completely healthy.

4. (XXXVII) A certain man from Friuli bemoaned the fact that he was deprived of the use of his tongue. Led by his mother, he came to blessed Anthony's ark. While he devoutly persisted in prayer before the tomb, he regained the gift of speech which he had lost for a long time.

36. - CONCERNING EPILEPTICS

1. (XXXVIII) In the city of Padua, there was a certain woman whose name was Michelotta. While she was suffering for eight days from a certain malady, she was also horribly taken by baneful falling sickness, completely lost the sight of both eyes, and seemed to be dying. 2. When her mother took her to the tomb of the saintly father Anthony and had her placed above the ark so that she could pray, her eyes suddenly opened and she received her eyesight again. From that time on, she no longer suffered from baneful epilepsy.

3. (XXXIX) A young boy, called Simon, as of three years had been tormented by attacks of falling sickness. Dropping forward, he would often dash his face against the ground. When he once suffered a bad fall, he began to shake so much as to arouse pity, and he could not move himself anywhere, despite his every effort. 4. Having made a vow, his solicitous mother led the boy to saint Anthony's

Camposampiero, Padua: The interior of the shrine was built in the first half of the fifteenth century.

When the inhabitants of Rimini refused to listen to St. Anthony, he preached to the fish along the seashore.

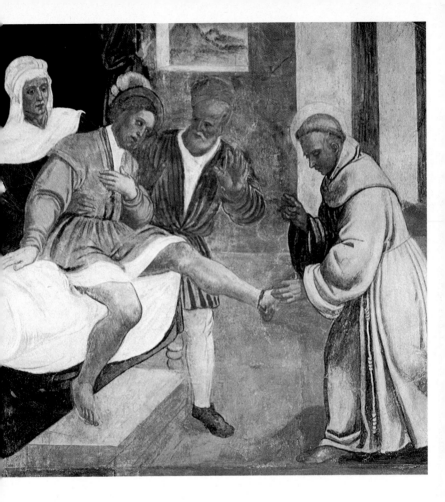

A young man, who had kicked at his mother, later cut off his foot in remorse. St. Anthony miraculously reattached the foot.

St. Anthony reconciles a family by having a newborn child speak out in defense of his mother's virtue.

With the sign of the cross, St. Anthony protects himself against the deadly effects of food poisoned by heretics.

Above the entrance to the church (interior): Mary with Child between St. Anthony and St. Jerome.

St. Anthony preaches from the nut tree (B. Pilati, sixteenth-century).

tomb. When she had prayed, they returned home, and the boy no longer gave even a sign of the above-mentioned infirmity.

37. - CONCERNING HUNCHBACKS

1. (XL) A certain youngster, whose name was Trentinus, since a bone grew in his spinal column, walked hunchbacked for five years, supporting himself on a crutch, and his hands drooped to his knees. 2. When his devout mother led him one day to saint Anthony's tomb, he was placed above the sepulchre. Since the hump immediately began to get smaller, he came down and, setting aside the crutch, went home, walking upright with his mother.

3. (XLI) In the city of Treviso, a woman, whose name was Veneziana, bore on her chest for more than two years a hump as large as a loaf of bread. When, for whatever reason, she walked anywhere, her head would tend to droop toward her knees. 4. Accordingly, when she came to the tomb of blessed Anthony, she prayed insistently for two days. Once her hump was leveled and her head lifted up, she returned home.

5. (XLII) When a certain man, whose name was Guidotto, was once suffering from a serious illnes, his kidneys were impaired and he developed a hump. He couldn't walk without the support of crutches and his head would droop almost to the ground. 6. When his mother had him led to blessed Anthony's sepulchre so that he might regain his health, he suddenly began to feel such great

pains throughout his whole body that he perspired violently because of his anguish. As the pain subsided, the man could distend his kidneys and immediately, through the saint's merits, the hump disappeared.

38. - CONCERNING THE FEVERISH

1. (XLIII) Bonzio of Roncaglia, when he suffered great pain during the course of eight days because of a swollen throat, began to feel a fiery fever as his distress became sharper. 2. One day, as two friars were passing the house where he lay, they went to visit him. When they had consoled him with the many things they said and had moved him to penance, one of them pulled out a piece of the mantle that blessed Anthony was accustomed to wear and placed it on the ailing man so that he might regain his health. 3. There and then, in the presence of the friars, he got well; and, feeling his own pulse, he noted that the fever had ceased. When the friars left, the sick man got up immediately and, having made with the piece of the mantle the sign of the cross on his head, the swelling of the throat disappeared.

4. (XLIV) A boy, called Zono, who became weak from quartan fever and suffered profoundly from a kind of gout, was brought to the tomb of the most saintly father Anthony. When he had remained for a short while above the ark where he had been placed, he came down freed from the gout and, at the same time, from the fever.

39. - CONCERNING
RESUSCITATIONS FROM THE DEAD

1. (XLV) In the town of Padua there was a small girl, called Eurilia, who as usual followed her mother as she went to a neighbour's house to ask for fire. When she was returning home, the mother found her daughter dead in a ditch full of water and mud, floating on her back with her face turned up. 2. As she rushed in, the weeping mother pulled out her drowned daughter from the water and placed her along the bank of the ditch, while many came running quickly to the sad spectacle. 3. A certain man who was among the bystanders, having noted that she was rigid because of the deadly cold, turned her head downward and raised her feet high above a table. But, even in this position, Eurilia did not make a sound nor give any sign of life, her cheeks remaining drawn and her lips closed like those of a dead person. Every hope of saving her was gone. 4. The anxious mother, however, making a vow to the Lord and to his servant, blessed Anthony, promised to bring a wax image to his tomb if he would deign to give her daughter back to her, alive. 5. As soon as she made the vow, the girl immediately moved her lips in the sight of all. When someone put his finger into her mouth, she threw up the water she had swallowed, and, through the saintly father's merits, regained her bodily temperature and came back to life.

6. (XLVI) Something similar happened in the city of Comacchio. There was a certain man called Dominic, who, as he left his home one day to do some work, had his small son accompany him, walk-

ing behind him. 7. When he had gone a little distance from his home, as he looked back, he saw no one. Worried, with stunned eyes, he went about searching all around. At last, he found his son, drowned in a lake. 8. The unfortunate father pulled him out and gave the dead boy to his mother. But she, immediately making a vow, received him alive through the merits of most blessed Anthony.

40. - CONCERNING THE UNBROKEN DRINKING GLASS

1. (XLVII) A certain knight of Salvaterra, called Aleardino, from early age was deceived by heretical perversity. One day, after the saint's death, he came to Padua with his wife and large family. While he was at table, he talked with the other guests about the miracles which were being granted to devout faithful through blessed Anthony's merits. 2. And, since all the others claimed that blessed Anthony was truly a saint of God, Aleardino, who had emptied a drinking glass which he held in his hand, exclaimed, more or less, in these words, «If the one, whom you claim to be a saint, will keep this glass from breaking, I will then believe to be true what you are trying to make me accept concerning him.» 3. And, from the place where he was sitting at table, he threw the drinking glass to the ground. Astonishing to say, the glass struck the stone floor, resisted and remained intact, in view of all those who were standing close by in the street.

4. When he saw the miracle, the knight was led to repent and quickly sprang up to pick up the unbroken glass. Bringing it with himself, he precise-

ly described to the friars everything that had happened. 5. Then, after he had confessed and devoutly accepted the penance imposed for his sins, he faithfully adhered to Christ and with utmost constancy proclaimed his miracles.

41. - CONCERNING THE WOMAN WHO WAS AFFLICTED AND THEN HEALED BY THE LORD

1. (XLVIII) A certain sister of the Order of the Poor Ladies, called Olive, when the saintly father's body still remained unburied, drew near to it with suppliant devotion to kiss his hand. 2. While she remained prostrate before the saintly body, she poured out her prayers to God and, among other things, suppliantly requested that, through the merits of most blessed father Anthony, the Lord cause her to suffer in the present life all the pain she deserved for her sins, without sparing any punishment for the future.

3. When she concluded her prayer, she reentered the monastery. Suddenly, a very powerful pain assailed her whole body and she couldn't hold herself up in any manner whatsoever. And, because of the violent distress of her pain, she also disturbed the other sisters with her loud cries. 4. The next day, when the others went to dine, she also sneaked in secretly. As her pain gradually grew in intensity, she couldn't take any food, but instead tossed about from one place to another, while the other sisters ate.

5. By order of the abbess, she was taken to the infirmary. And she, who had asked with all her longing to be afflicted with punishment in the present life, now begged with ever increasing prayers

for a remedy. 6. At last, when she remembered that she had kept a piece of saint Anthony's habit, she had it brought to her, at once applied it to herself, and every pain immediately left her.

42. - CONCERNING THE WOMAN WHO THREW HERSELF INTO A RIVER BUT REMAINED DRY

1. (XLIX) A certain woman from Monselice, religious from her childhood because of her devout faith, was legally bound in marriage to a certain man who lived only according to carnal desire. 2. He—according to what is written: a husband is sanctified through his faithful wife[1] —because of her entreaties, one day went to a priest and confessed his sins. When he returned home, he solemnly promised that he would go to visit the tomb of St. James and that he would have his wife come with him. 3. Made quite happy by this, the wife hastened her journey as quickly as she could and, with her entreaties, induced her husband to go to the city of Padua in order to buy what was necessary for the pilgrimage.

4. When they set out, joined by fellow wayfarers, they continued along the road which leads to Padua. The wife, not being able to hide her interior joy and breaking out in laughter and external merriment, manifested her heartfelt joy with uncommon cheerfulness. 5. When her husband saw this, becoming impatient with such excessive exultation, he said to her, «Why, deceived by the vain hope of departing, are you happily oozing with so much babbling and breaking out in laughter and unsuitable

---

[1] See 1 Corinthians 7:14.

gestures? Be it known to you that I have changed my mind and by no means will I go where you are hurrying.»

6. When she heard these words, the woman suddenly became pale and showed by her changed expression that she was saddened. And, since her husband persisted in exasperating her with words of this kind, after a long silence, she at last answered the scolder, «If you do not in fact fulfill the obligation of the pilgrimage that you promised me, in the name of Jesus Christ and of blessed Anthony, know that I will drown myself.» 7. But he gave no credence at all to her words, and, what is more, with a hardened expression on his face and calling her foolish, he firmly denied that he would fulfill his promise. 8. The sad woman, when all hope was taken away from her and her trust was completely rendered vain, gave in to her self-destructiveness and, invoking the name of blessed Anthony, threw herself into the river which flowed along the road.

9. When the other women who were present saw her being tossed about in the midst of the flowing river, they were initially made breathless by the shock, but then hastened to her as quickly as possible. Forgetful of their feminine sense of shame and getting themselves wet up to their waistlines with all their garments, they pulled her out of the water that had covered her completely. 10. When she was pulled out, and they had placed her along the bank—I narrate what is truly marvelous!—it was found that not even a thread of her undergarment was wet, whereas the women who had saved her were wringing out their clothes to force the excessive quantity of water out of them.

11. Indeed, one can understand, as Scripture testifies, «may the Lord protect those who walk in simplicity.»[1] Nevertheless, we do not propose that a fact of this kind be imitated, for what was done we attribute more readily to foolishness than to virtue. But we do certainly believe that the merits of the most saintly father, who was invoked by the woman, obtained this from God; and, truly, we do not doubt that he was always zealous for the virtue of simplicity.

43. - CONCERNING THE LOST AT SEA

1. (L) By chance one day, a group of men and women, almost twenty-six in number, boarded a boat at Saint Hilary to go to Venice. While they were sailing, propelled by oars, they reached at the hour of Compline the spot in the lagoon which is not quite distant from the Church of Saint George in Alga. Since a furious storm broke out, they tried to find refuge at that place, but, as the tempest grew worse, they were carried to an entirely unknown spot.

2. Since they couldn't see each other and the wind and rain violently descended on them from above, they thoroughly despaired of being saved and desired that their imminent death be hastened and their anxiety ended with their lives. Thus, they all wept, and quite increased the noise of the gale with their shrill shouting. 3. Having, therefore, confessed their sins and received absolution from a priest who was with them, they began to invoke beseechingly the intercession of blessed Anthony and

---

[1] See Proverbs 2:7.

to bind themselves by promises to him. 4. Some pledged to give a boat made of wax; others resolved to surround the saintly father's ark with wax candles.

5. No sooner did they finish making their promises when the gale immediately subsided around them. But, since it was still dark, no one knew where they were or where they were heading. 6. And, behold, from the boat in which they were, a kind of light came out and preceded them as they sailed, making them weep for joy. Offering itself as a guide, it led them safely to the place of Saint Mark the Little, a mile from Venice. 7. Torn from the hand of death through the merits of blessed Anthony, when they reached the place, the light which continually led them during the journey disappeared and, after it brought them to safety, thereafter hid its bright rays. 8. At last they said that, while they cut through the becalmed sea, guided by the light, although they tried with the oars to hold back the boat which sailed at great speed, they could do nothing at all until they reached the desired port on the coast, led by the light which preceded them.

44. - CONCERNING THE DISBELIEVER
WHO WAS PUNISHED AND HEALED

1. (LI) One day, when a churchman from Anguillara, called Guidotto, was in a room of the lord bishop of Padua, he secretly scoffed at the witnesses who were giving testimony about blessed Anthony's miracles. The next night, he began to be assailed by a powerful pain throughout his body, so much so that he began to think his mortal judgment was, without doubt, imminent.

2. Rightly considering himself unworthy of mercy, he therefore began to ask his mother to make a promise, in his name, to God's saint so that he might merit to receive forgiveness. 3. When she made the promise, the pain immediately ceased and he was healed before daybreak. And, the one who had mocked the witnesses with the scoffing of his disbelief was himself compelled to bear testimony to the truth.

45. - CONCERNING THE MILLET
SPARED FROM SPARROWS

1. (LII) A certain woman from Tremignon, called Vita, when she was aflame with great devotion to blessed Anthony, longed eagerly and with utmost desire to come to his sepulchre. 2. But, since harvest tide was approaching and countless sparrows were ravaging the millet, which was already white and ready to be gathered, she was appointed to watch over the crop in order to keep in flight that troublesome species of birds. Thus, on no occasion, could she find the opportunity to come to the tomb.

3. One day, therefore, as she came to the enclosure which surrounded the millet, she promised that, if blessed Anthony guarded it from the sparrows, she would visit his sepulchre nine times. 4. Having made the promise, the great number of birds suddenly quit the place, as if one united army, and not even a sparrow, as she could see, remained on the willows which surrounded the millet.

46. - CONCERNING THE UNFULFILLED PROMISE

1. (LIII) A certain boy from the city of Padua, called Henry, when his neck became swollen, suffered great pain for fifteen days. His mother promised to bring a wax reproduction of a head with a neck to saint Anthony's tomb. When the boy returned from the friars' place, his neck was cured. 2. But, since the boy's mother was unfaithful to what she said and did not fulfill her promise, his neck again began to swell.

3. Then, conscious of her fault, the woman rightly became sorrowful and, having renewed her promise, had a waxen head with a neck taken to the saint's sepulchre. 4. As soon as this was done, the swollen neck immediately became normal, and, when a few days had passed, the boy healed completely, through Our Lord Jesus Christ, to whom is all honour and glory eternally, for ever and ever. Amen.

47. - CONCLUSION TO THE BOOK OF MIRACLES

1. Indeed, the Lord of majesty deigned to work through his servant Anthony many other signs which are not written in this book.[1] 2. Here we have gathered a few from among many, choosing from the better known those that are most certain, in order to give an opportunity to others, who may wish to do so, to add to these praises. And, not assenting to what is uncertain, while we intend to praise the saint, may we guard our tongues from the vice of lying. 3. Truly, if his miraculous signs,

---

[1] See John 20:30.

some of which are great, and his marvels, which are extraordinary, were described one by one, I am afraid that just as their number might cause discomfort to the reader so also the unusual greatness of the works might give rise to the danger of disbelief in the minds of the weak.

FINAL PRAYER TO THE SAINT

4. Behold, most benign father, I have narrated your deeds, putting them in writing in some manner, even if with clumsy words. Behold, speaking according to my available information, I have announced your true greatness, even if not fully.

5. I beseech you, pious father, remember me with all the other friars of your order. You, because of your happy destiny and immortal state, stand at the throne of God. Through your merits, draw those who long to be with you from the valley of misery and from the mire of rejection.

6. Remember, I say, the deep mercy you showed towards the wretched while you were still alive in the flesh, although you yourself did not live carnally. And, united to the Source of mercy, may you draw torrent of bliss to pour forth on those who are thirsting a stream of grace. Amen.

HERE END THE LIFE AND MIRACLES OF SAINT ANTHONY THE CONFESSOR